I0024743

Sustainable Reintegration of Returning Migrants

A BETTER HOMECOMING

OECD

BETTER POLICIES FOR BETTER LIVES

This work is published under the responsibility of the Secretary-General of the OECD. The opinions expressed and arguments employed herein do not necessarily reflect the official views of OECD member countries.

This document, as well as any data and map included herein, are without prejudice to the status of or sovereignty over any territory, to the delimitation of international frontiers and boundaries and to the name of any territory, city or area.

The statistical data for Israel are supplied by and under the responsibility of the relevant Israeli authorities. The use of such data by the OECD is without prejudice to the status of the Golan Heights, East Jerusalem and Israeli settlements in the West Bank under the terms of international law.

Note by Turkey
The information in this document with reference to "Cyprus" relates to the southern part of the Island. There is no single authority representing both Turkish and Greek Cypriot people on the Island. Turkey recognises the Turkish Republic of Northern Cyprus (TRNC). Until a lasting and equitable solution is found within the context of the United Nations, Turkey shall preserve its position concerning the "Cyprus issue".

Note by all the European Union Member States of the OECD and the European Union
The Republic of Cyprus is recognised by all members of the United Nations with the exception of Turkey. The information in this document relates to the area under the effective control of the Government of the Republic of Cyprus.

Please cite this publication as:
OECD (2020), *Sustainable Reintegration of Returning Migrants: A Better Homecoming*, OECD Publishing, Paris, *https://doi.org/10.1787/5fee55b3-en*.

ISBN 978-92-64-79669-0 (print)
ISBN 978-92-64-64991-0 (pdf)

Photo credits: Cover © Icons Market/Shutterstock.com.

Corrigenda to publications may be found on line at: *www.oecd.org/about/publishing/corrigenda.htm*.
© OECD 2020

The use of this work, whether digital or print, is governed by the Terms and Conditions to be found at *http://www.oecd.org/termsandconditions*.

Foreword

To explore how to improve the sustainability of reintegration programmes, drawing on current experience, and contribute to the understanding of how to monitor and evaluate such programmes, the OECD Secretariat, with support from the German Corporation for International Cooperation (Deutsche Gesellschaft für Internationale Zusammenarbeit GmbH – GIZ), commissioned by the Federal Ministry for Economic Cooperation and Development, organised a peer-learning exercise in 2019 and 2020. From June 2019 through February 2020, the OECD Secretariat, along with project partners from both interior and development ministries of eight European countries, participated in Study Visits in different European countries (Switzerland, France, United Kingdom, Belgium, Germany, Denmark, Sweden and Norway) and in origin countries (Tunisia, Kosovo and Senegal). The visits encompassed the EU level; European OECD countries (Bern, Paris, London, Brussels, Berlin, Copenhagen, Malmö and Oslo); and origin countries (Tunis, Pristina, Dakar). In total, more than 100 stakeholders participated in the study tours, presenting and discussing programme objectives, design and outcomes. The findings have been further informed by the involvement of other actors, including potential returnees and returnees, diaspora organisations and civil society. The OECD also conducted analyses of specific return corridors.

The report includes the findings of these study tours. Initial project findings were discussed in a series of workshops in June 2020 with project partners and additional participants including scholars and representatives of international organisations. An earlier version of the study findings was presented at the OECD Working Party on Migration in June 2020.

Acknowledgements

This report was written by an OECD Secretariat team led by Jonathan Chaloff. The report draws on 11 interactive study tours organised in collaboration with the Swiss State Secretariat for Migration, the French Office for Immigration and Integration (OFII), the Home Office and DfID in the United Kingdom, Fedasil in Belgium, BMZ, BMI and GIZ in Germany, the Ministry of Immigration and Integration and Ministry of Foreign Affairs in Denmark, the Swedish Migration Agency and DELMI in Sweden, and UDI in Norway. GIZ and OFII partnered in organising study tours in Tunisia, Kosovo and Senegal. IOM participated in all the study tours and workshops. The participants from governments, international organisations, civil society and research are too numerous to mention individually. Support for organising these study tours and the workshops, as well as research support, was provided by Shirin Abrishami Kashani, Maria Vincenza Desiderio, Nicole Fusi and Adam Hussain. Background reports on origin countries were drafted by Samuel Hall, Eleonora Castagnone, Anna Ferro, Hélène Hammouda, Edith Arrat and Safet Fazliu. The OECD Secretariat would like to thank the German Corporation for International Cooperation (Deutsche Gesellschaft für Internationale Zusammenarbeit GmbH – GIZ), commissioned by the Federal Ministry for Economic Cooperation and Development, for support for the project and for commenting on drafts of this report. Delegates to the OECD Working Party on Migration also provided comments.

Table of contents

Follow OECD Publications on:

http://twitter.com/OECD_Pubs

http://www.facebook.com/OECDPublications

http://www.linkedin.com/groups/OECD-Publications-4645871

http://www.youtube.com/oecdilibrary

http://www.oecd.org/oecddirect/

Acronyms and Abbreviations

AFD	French Development Agency (Agence Française de Développement)
AHK	German Chambers of Commerce Abroad
ANETI	National Employment and Self-Employment Agency, Tunisia (Agence Nationale pour l'Emploi et le Travail Indépendant)
AVR	Assisted Voluntary Return
AVRR	Assisted Voluntary Return and Reintegration
BAMF	Federal Office for Migration and Refugees
BMI	Federal Ministry of Interior, Community and Building
BMZ	Federal Ministry for Cooperation and Development
CSO	Civil society organisation
DFID	United Kingdom Department for International Development
DIMAK	German Information Centre for Migration, Training and Career, Kosovo
DiREC	Displacement and Returnees Executive Committee
DRC	Danish Refugee Council
ENABEL	Belgian development agency
ERRIN	European Return and Reintegration Network
ERSO	European Reintegration Support Organizations network
FAC	Federal Asylum Centre
FCDO	Foreign, Commonwealth and Development Office
FCO	United Kingdom Foreign and Commonwealth Office
Fedasil	Belgian Federal Agency for the Reception of Asylum Seekers
GARP	Government Assisted Repatriation Program in Germany
GIZ	German Corporation for International Cooperation (Deutsche Gesellschaft für Internationale Zusammenarbeit)
IAF	Inter-American Foundation
IMZ	Swiss Inter-Ministerial Cooperation Structure
IOM	International Organization for Migration
MEASURE	Mediterranean Sustainable Integration project

NOAS	Norwegian Organisation for Asylum Seekers
NORAD	Norwegian Agency for Development Cooperation
ODA	Official development assistance
OECD	Organisation for Economic Co-operation and Development
OFII	French Office for Immigration and Integration
OQTF	Order to leave French territory
RCS	Return Counselling Services
REAG	Reintegration and Emigration Program for Asylum-Seekers in Germany
RIAT	Transition to Reintegration Assistance Tool
SDC	Swiss Agency for Development and Cooperation
SEM	Federal Department for Justice and Police, Swiss Secretariat for Migration
SMA	Swedish Migration Agency
TEMPER	Temporary Versus Permanent Migration Project
UDI	Norwegian Directorate of Immigration
VRS	Voluntary Return Services

Executive summary

The question of how to ensure the safe and dignified return to their origin countries of migrants who do not have grounds to remain is a key question for many OECD countries. Alongside removal, return and reintegration assistance have become an integral part of migration management in many OECD countries. Offering opportunities to take assisted return is seen as a means of increasing returns at a lower cost. Providing reintegration assistance after return is both an incentive to use this channel and a means of reducing the risk of illegal remigration. Supporting return for all migrants who wish to do so – including legally resident migrants – can reinforce migration management. At the same time, development cooperation includes increasing activity to support the capacity of countries of origin to reintegrate returning migrants.

This report examines factors which contribute to improve sustainability of reintegration at the individual level and at the programme level. It situates reintegration assistance as an incentive in the understanding of the drivers of return migration. While assistance is not alone a sufficient incentive to return, a return and reintegration programme which builds a perspective on return can make a difference in the decision process and help build a more sustainable individual outcome, whether it involves a revenue-generating activity or social reintegration into the home community. It identifies some of the key elements of an effective individual reintegration programme, including outreach and counselling, case management and referral, and partnerships.

The sustainability of reintegration goes beyond the individual. Programmes must respond to a number of objectives, including increasing and accelerating returns of persons subject to removal, preventing the creation of pull factors, protecting relations with origin countries, coherence with development objectives, and meeting national and international obligations. The individual case work approach, with better targeting of key categories, can help improve sustainability of programmes. The current monitoring framework is focused on project indicators and beneficiary outcomes, and is inadequate to assess the broader impact of initiatives. The report proposes a number of points to reinforce in programme design and in evaluation and monitoring, indicating areas for mutualisation of efforts among countries in implementation and coordination with origin countries.

1 Introduction

This chapter presents the main findings of a multi-country peer review study involving eight European OECD countries and actors from migration and development authorities, as well as partners in both origin and destination countries implementing and supporting reintegration programmes for migrants returning home. Reintegration assistance has been added to the policy toolbox for managing migration to respond to different objectives, including increasing uptake of voluntary return and ensuring a safe and dignified return. The chapter reviews programme design and implementation, noting the need for coordination and a broader evaluation framework.

Migration is a complex and multi-directional process: it can be short-term, permanent, circular, and in some cases, eventually end in return. Return can be the natural result of a migration project coming to an end – often, however, returns occur involuntarily through removal, or against the background of a lack of opportunities and difficult experiences in the destination country, sometimes combined with the threat of removal. Whether those who are not granted residence permits or who do not fall under international protection actually leave the country has implications for the integrity of regular migration pathways – the asylum system in particular.

Considering the difficult circumstances under which many migrants return and the difficult labour market conditions, stigma, and often fragile conditions awaiting them in their origin countries, actors in the return process are increasingly seeking to support return migrants beyond their re-entry in the origin country. The first consideration is to enhance returns and to reduce the chance that returnees remigrate irregularly. In parallel, countries seeking to return migrants want to set incentives and signals to discourage irregular entry of other migrants. A further consideration is to try to minimise cost – striking a balance between the cost of reintegration and the financial benefits associated with substituting removals. For migrants who hold legal residence in the host country, supporting return and reintegration can be a means of contributing to the development of the origin country and ensuring that the migration project of the individual is successfully realised. At the same time, reintegration assistance seeks to prevent returns, regardless of scale, from overwhelming local infrastructure and undermining social cohesion in the origin country. Increasing attention to returnees' reintegration needs partly stems from the realisation that the feasibility and legitimacy of return policies and practices depend on the sustainable reintegration of individual returnees into their origin communities. Complementing return assistance with reintegration support programmes is meant to improve returnees' inclusion – or re-inclusion – in origin country societies and allow them to contribute to their home communities. Inclusion, development and a reduction in migration out of desperation is an objective on which different partners can agree: destination countries, origin countries and returning migrants themselves.

The findings contained in this report, summarised in the following section, are drawn from a multi-partner peer review study involving eight OECD countries and site visits in 11 different locations (Box 1.1).

Box 1.1. The peer review study on Return and Reintegration: Maximising Sustainability

The peer-learning exercise organised and facilitated by the OECD Secretariat brought together participants from interior and development ministries of eight European countries (Switzerland, France, United Kingdom, Belgium, Germany, Denmark, Sweden and Norway). Visits to the services running return and reintegration programmes in each country – including partners providing counselling, orientation and other pre-return support – were supplemented with visits to Tunisia, Kosovo and Senegal. The two-day visits involved exchanges among officials, partners and returning migrants, giving participants a chance to share experiences and practices. Additional consultations took place in a series of workshops held in June 2020, open to other countries and organisations. Further background material for the project was provided for six countries of origin (Afghanistan, Iraq, Tunisia, Senegal, Nigeria and Kosovo).

1.1. Main findings

1.1.1. The past five years have seen return move up the policy agenda in OECD countries, especially in Europe

Over the past five years, large-scale displacements of people fleeing war-torn zones, natural disasters or economically deprived areas have put increasing pressure on receiving countries and regions. While most of the flows have been towards non-OECD countries, inflows of asylum seekers to OECD countries spiked in 2015, marking a record, before declining. While a large share of asylum seekers received some form of international protection, a significant number of requests did not lead to a positive response. As a result, a number of OECD countries have seen the population of migrants without a lawful residence permit and required to return increase, especially when irregular migration inflows outside the asylum system are also considered. In most countries concerned, particularly in Europe, returns have not kept pace with this increase. As a result, policy attention has given more attention to approaches and measures to support returns. Alongside enforcement and compliance measures, assisted return initiatives have evolved.

1.1.2. Reintegration assistance has expanded and became part of the policy toolbox for return

Assisted return has long been available for some categories of migrants, such as asylum seekers who withdraw or are refused their asylum request and refugees for whom the situation in the origin country allows return. While return assistance used to be limited to travel support and limited spending money, recent years have seen the development of reintegration assistance, which provides cash and in-kind support following return to the origin country. These programmes, largely but not exclusively run by Ministries of the Interior through co-ordinating bodies, share common features in terms of design. In numerical terms, they remain niche initiatives (a relatively small number of all return migrants participate), but have taken on importance as a solution for certain target groups, and in light of possible increases in the number of returns.

Not all OECD countries have chosen to offer return and reintegration support. The United States does not offer return or reintegration assistance, for example, relying on other policy mechanisms to promote returns. Canada had a pilot in the early 2010s, but has not offered support since then. Australia and Israel offer programmes to specific target groups. In contrast, European countries offer programmes, through national and EU programmes, and reintegration assistance is a key part of policy at both national and EU level in Europe.

1.1.3. This has been mirrored by growing emphasis on reintegration programmes in origin countries

As return migration to many origin countries increases, development cooperation has reflected this growing importance. For many donor countries, facilitating returns has long included policy goals such as greater co-operation on returns, through readmission agreements and protocols; it now sees priority also given to support the capacity of origin countries to reintegrate returning migrants. The development cooperation reintegration programmes in origin countries are distinct from those offering individual return and reintegration support. Such programmes tend to be community-based, with broader eligibility open to migrants who returned outside of any programme, including migrants who returned from third countries, forced returns and spontaneous returns. Germany's programmes also serve the local population – regardless of any migration experience. Individual support packages can be difficult to align with a general development perspective, but in-kind support may build capacity of public and non-governmental origin country institutions charged with achieving general development objectives. Further, individual reintegration assistance can buy into development programmes and provide additional resources to which mainstream services can orient beneficiaries. This requires each programme to be aware of the services provided by the other, and an effective referral and collaboration mechanism. In the projects reviewed, in spite of substantial progress, bridging between these services was often incomplete. National liaisons and EU representation are key in ensuring links.

1.1.4. The rationale for providing assistance for voluntary return and reintegration is similar across countries

Assisted return and reintegration programmes largely aim to increase and facilitate the return and re-establishment in the origin country of persons who might otherwise be subject to removal or who do not yet have a right to remain. In countries which offer programmes, assisted return and reintegration of this group is seen as preferable to forced return, for economic, political and humanitarian considerations. The economic consideration is often the first reason for providing incentives to accept voluntary return, since it obviates the need for detention, escort and other costly measures associated with removal. What is more, even when public opinion supports a strict removal policy, individual removals may elicit a negative public reaction. Assisted return addresses this concern and also provides a safer and more dignified alternative to forced return. In this sense, it is often in line with both international commitments and national principles.

The introduction of assisted return combined with subsequent reintegration has been associated with more and easier return, although many other factors affect return decisions: the individual situation of the migrant, the economic, social and political circumstances in the origin country, the opportunities to remain in the destination country, etc. The many factors involved make changes in return numbers difficult to link directly to the availability of assistance, and thus hamper a proper evaluation of these programmes.

1.1.5. Reconciling individual assistance programmes with development assistance objectives remains a challenge

The multiple objectives of return and assisted reintegration programmes are reflected in a push in many European countries towards a whole-of-government approach in their organisation, especially coordination between Ministries of Interior and development cooperation agencies. This is reflected in policy documents but has met with some difficulty in translation to programme implementation. Individual reintegration assistance grants to voluntary returnees are generally part of policy for management of migration. Individual assistance contrasts with the development practice of supporting communities, infrastructure and broader capacity in the country of origin. At the individual level, reintegration assistance is not targeted to the most needy, or the most qualified, but to those who are eligible due to their status in the destination country. One response to attempt to reconcile these approaches has been to design reintegration assistance to work through, and reinforce, structures and services which are available to all returning migrants and the local population in general.

1.1.6. Most migrants returning do not receive reintegration assistance

In origin countries, most returns – even voluntary returns – are not assisted and most migrants do not receive return assistance. In part this is because many returns are from countries which do not offer assistance; in Africa, for example, intra-regional migration exceeds returns from Europe. Some reintegration support may be offered for returns in this case – for example, through the EU-IOM Joint Initiative. Forced returns are significant – and outnumber assisted returns in most countries – but generally ineligible for reintegration assistance as part of the return process. Migrants who were removed may be eligible for some forms of reintegration assistance offered in the origin country after they have returned, but this eligibility appears usually only to be discovered after return.

At the same time, many of those eligible for assistance do not return, and most returnees who are eligible nonetheless return without the package. The fact that reintegration assistance is available is not enough to bring about a return decision, and many returnees note that the reintegration assistance was not the driving factor behind their return. Even with information provided during the asylum process and at points of contact with potential beneficiaries, many remain unaware of reintegration assistance. Others may know of reintegration assistance but prefer to return without taking the package, to remain invisible to origin country authorities, to facilitate future attempts at migration or because they see the reintegration assistance as too complex or ill-suited for their individual project. Further, return decisions often occur suddenly, leaving little time to organise reintegration assistance prior to return.

The number of returnees with reintegration packages adds up to a significant total: for example, more than 15 000 in Germany and 2 600 in France in 2018. Nonetheless, the low uptake relative to eligibility is surprising, as reintegration assistance enhances the available resources – both financial and non-financial – of the beneficiaries who are able to use it as part of a project of re-establishment in the origin country.

1.1.7. Offering reintegration assistance alone is not enough to drive a return decision

The cash amount or equivalent value of in-kind reintegration assistance offered to returning migrants varies. The presence of the assistance, and its amount, do not appear to be the main consideration in the return decision, as other factors are more important. However, it is a factor in the return decision, especially when counselling about return can refer to a package available to effectively support a return project.

The criteria used to set the amount vary among the countries examined, over time, and according to eligibility criteria. A concern is whether potential benefits may be a pull factor. As a consequence, migrants for whom barriers on entry are low (e.g. geographical proximity or visa-free admission) are usually not eligible for larger reintegration support. For other migrants, the costs of migration exceed any assistance they might receive; further, reintegration assistance offered through in-kind packages include a range of support, over time, making it hard for potential beneficiaries to calculate their cash equivalent, reducing the risk of them being a pull factor. International "package-shopping" for the most favourable assistance has not been detected, although there is no system for direct information exchange across countries to identify any migrants who might apply for assistance from different countries over time, including in origin countries. In contrast, some countries have systems in place to monitor use of return assistance programmes to reduce cash and travel benefits accordingly if pull factors are suspected.

1.1.8. Return counselling can encourage uptake of assisted return

Most potential returnees under reintegration assistance programmes do not initially consider return as an acceptable option, as they are focused on remaining and realising their migration project. While standardised information is provided at different points in the asylum process, a casework approach, addressing individual psychological states of mind at different points of the decision-making process, appears to be most effective. The timing and form of providing return information seems to be of particular importance. For asylum seekers, a crucial moment is when they receive the final decision. While some countries inform applicants by mail, in-person delivery of final decisions gives an opportunity to present return options with a better chance of being heard.

To shift the perception of return and frame it as an opportunity and not a failure, several techniques have been successful, including the "motivational interview technique", which emphasises the chance to take control over one's personal life. Return counselling involves painting a picture of possibilities after return; this can be based on individual counselling but can also be supported with testimony of successful return, through direct contact with previous returnees or material such as narrative films recounting their experience.

1.1.9. Trusted counsellors and mediators can motivate return for some

Counselling in the enforcement context – such as detention, reporting and even reception centres – by actors associated with enforcement is less successful in fostering interest in voluntary return and reintegration than information and counselling by trusted figures in neutral contexts. Separating return counselling – physically and procedurally – from enforcement and legal proceedings tends to be more effective. Involving stakeholders such as cultural and religious community figures, diaspora organisations and former returnees allows for a more convincing case. Involvement can take the form of formal recruitment, but also training and awareness raising. For unaccompanied minors, this may mean tutors or teachers; for victims of trafficking, it may mean their case workers. While partnering with civil society can help make the case for return more compelling, these actors cannot be expected to promote return in all cases, since they may not see it as the best option for some individuals. Contracting civil society organisations and other non-governmental actors thus requires accepting that some eligible beneficiaries will not be advised to return; public actors must continue to provide information and counselling based on the legal obligation to return.

1.1.10. Contact with the origin country can help develop a perspective on return

The longer migrants have been abroad, the less they know about the situation and opportunities in their home country. To address this, most countries covered in this review have included links to experts on the home country, including videoconferences, mediators, informational visits, and other forms of direct contact in order to inform potential returnees of structures and offers available upon return and develop a concrete vision of post-return life. Not all counsellors have knowledge about origin countries, let alone an identified roster of contacts in the home country. One successful way to address this gap is to use intermediating bodies to make the connection between host country counsellors and contacts in the origin country who are familiar with the situation. This is one task of the Reintegration Scouts in Germany. In some cases, the counterpart is the implementing partner or contact who would eventually receive the case or collaborate in a reintegration plan prior to return. Fedasil organises annual meetings between operators in Belgium and origin countries to strengthen such contacts.

1.1.11. Different but coherent forms of outreach are necessary

Campaigns to encourage uptake of voluntary return can be misperceived as targeting resident communities. As a baseline, most countries have dedicated voluntary return websites with information – sometimes targeted only at intermediaries rather than at migrants – and hotlines for information are widely used. These are essential infrastructure for promoting voluntary return by providing clear information and success stories. Targeted social media campaigns have been effective in reaching specific groups of beneficiaries. Actors such as social workers, legal aides, and appointed guardians are key contacts for many potential returnees, especially asylum seekers and unaccompanied children. Nonetheless, their role as support may mean they have seen return as a negative outcome. Even public sector actors may be inclined negatively against considering return, especially for asylum seekers whose case has not reached a final decision. It can be difficult to shift perceptions of potential returnees if they receive mixed messages.

1.1.12. Preparation for return can improve prospects for reintegration

Returnees who have started their reintegration project prior to return appear to fare better, even though most must adjust their projects and expectations to adapt to the post-return reality. One factor is training. Skills development prior to return is identified as helpful, although most programmes allow only a limited time for counselling, let alone training. Preparing for return tends to be particularly difficult for asylum seekers who are employed or involved in integration programmes while awaiting a decision. While asylum seekers likely to stay should prepare for integration, others unlikely to have a positive outcome may find it harder to consider return when such investment in remaining is underway. Basic and short modules are compatible with supporting early integration while still contributing to later promotion of return. Modules experimented in Switzerland and Germany, for example, have focused on general skills of broad application (digital skills, financial literacy, operation of equipment, hygiene principles, etc.) Such dual intent training can take place even when the participants have not yet considered or chosen to use return and reintegration assistance.

1.1.13. Reintegration assistance packages involve many actors and partners…

The kind of assistance offered (skills development, psychosocial support etc.) and the monetary value of reintegration packages varies among countries, according to beneficiaries and over time. Nonetheless, programmes require multiple actors in the destination and origin country.

Partners which tend to be important for reintegration assistance include:

- Partners capable of providing skills assessment and labour market orientation, including assessment and (where relevant) certification of skills acquired abroad
- Entrepreneurial support structures, including development of a business plan, access to credit, mentoring, business networks and market information
- Social support services, including those working with populations with specific vulnerabilities, and those capable of supporting reinsertion of children in school or with health issues

In addition to partners essential for the implementation of programmes, other partners can contribute to reinforce the overall framework:

- Private sector actors, especially those seeking specific skills and competences of returning migrants
- Diaspora organisations can help identify reintegration opportunities, networks and investment and destigmatise return, although they may be reluctant to support initiatives associated with forced return. Diaspora associations can improve circulation of information on programmes in both the host and origin country – amplifying the impact of success but also of failed returns.
- Associations of returnees in particular can assist in orienting returning migrants and making them feel part of a community.
- Local actors (committees, cooperatives and councils, as well as regional offices of public services) can help provide support to returnees far from the capitals where donor-sponsored services are often centralised. Local councils can also help shift the narrative around return migration and create reintegration opportunities outside the capital region

1.1.14. …complicating coordination

Multiple partners, however, complicate oversight for the coordinator. The coordinator may be the sending country public body – in some cases, such as France's OFII, represented in countries of origin – or through an implementing partner co-ordinating the intervention in the origin country. This can be NGOs active in the country – for example, Belgium's Fedasil may work with Caritas, while Denmark may work with the Danish Refugee Council. This contact must however continually authorise projects, services, and changes in individual plans. While many countries take advantage of IOM's global presence to coordinate reintegration assistance, there is no single model. The central coordinating mechanism or partnership, or state-led model depends on a range of factors, including the institutional capacity of the destination and origin country, the needs of the individual returnee and the experience and expertise of the partner.

As the number of partners increases, coordination becomes more challenging not only in terms of accountability, data management and reporting, tender management and financial control, but also regarding ensuring continuity and referral. For return migrants, multiple interlocutors can be confusing; without a strong referral mechanism, there is a risk of duplication and blurring of responsibility.

No single model for coordination has emerged, beyond the transfer to an origin-country case manager following return. In the best of cases, when the local institutions are strong enough, projects can transfer case management to state institutions relatively quickly, providing accompanying measures and support. In cases where local institutions are weaker, the implementing partner has to maintain its role or find alternative structures. Individual reintegration support packages end – the typical horizon of support is 12 months. This end of support means a sometimes difficult rupture with the beneficiary. It can also be difficult to separate for the partners working closely with them and with which they have formed a relationship.

1.1.15. A whole of government approach also needs to be taken in the origin country

Although favouring returns and sustainable reintegration is among the policy priorities for many European countries cooperating with origin countries, reintegration assistance sometimes occurs outside of development assistance frameworks and independent of other diplomatic initiatives. To address this, liaison officers within embassies, regular meetings and key contact points appear to have been effective, especially with respect to the identification of shared objectives and areas for collaboration.

As reintegration assistance in many cases grew out of return assistance, in which origin countries were often not involved, co-ordination with origin-country institutions has expanded along with the programmes themselves. Direct transfer of cases and resources for reintegration assistance to origin country institutions remains unusual, although a hybrid model is emerging of contributing resources for specific services, and co-ordinating case intervention, with the origin country. In addition to identifying and partnering with relevant public bodies, reintegration assistance also requires to work with local communities to which migrants return, including regional and local offices, local officials and organisations.

Multiple donors supporting different reintegration assistance programmes and packages with varying amounts and eligibility criteria may result in overlap. To address this, coordination among different development actors active in the origin country to identify initiatives, increase uptake, avoid duplication and mutualise efforts has been undertaken by donors, for example in Senegal. Coordination includes national and EU actors, as well as public, NGO and international organisations working as project implementers. Liaison officers from destination countries and from the EU have a potentially larger role to play.

1.1.16. Reintegration packages alone cannot sustain infrastructure to support returning migrants in the origin country

A fee-for-services model, paid for by the host country, lies behind most individual reintegration assistance, even when it involves public services in the origin country. While individual support packages are time-limited and cover only a fraction of returning migrants, they are a resource input into an ecosystem of actors providing a range of services and affect the development of this ecosystem, giving actors more experience in working with return migrants. The number of beneficiaries receiving reintegration assistance is usually not large enough to drive an entire infrastructure. Using the packages to improve broader capacity of state, non-state, development co-operation actors and local institutions is essential for longer term sustainability of reintegration. Most reintegration programmes reviewed in this report, for example, contributed to fostering expertise in business development consultants, expanding contacts between private sector actors and civil society and strengthening the information exchange platform among participants. While not directly aiming at this result, they also contribute to cultivate a pool of local staff capable of conducting monitoring and evaluation to international standards, the longer-term development is necessary because partnerships for addressing short-term needs of returning migrants – reinsertion, business start-up, orientation – are not the same as those necessary to build medium and long term opportunities.

1.1.17. Livelihood assistance usually requires an individual project

The limited formal employment sector in many origin countries means that most reintegration projects aim for self-employment, involving development of a business plan. Projects developed prior to return often need to be reformulated or replaced after return to adapt to the situation. This requires better communication regarding the origin country. Even when this is in place, returnees often discover that their project is not feasible as imagined. A traditional roster of return activities, sometimes gendered, facilitates project management but does not necessarily respond to the motivation of the returnee. The need for flexibility to adapt to circumstances sometimes clashes with reporting and accounting requirements as well as the usual 12-month horizon for support. Success of enterprises depends on many factors beyond the amount of reintegration assistance. Returning migrants have skills which are often neglected, unacknowledged or uncertified. Skills both technical and soft acquired during migration can be of use after return. Skills assessment and – where relevant – certification can help not only guide entrepreneurial projects but also to access formal employment. Chambers of Commerce uniting employers from the destination country are an effective partner; GIZ, for example, works with German Chambers of Commerce in the origin country.

1.1.18. Changing the perception of returnees in the origin country can facilitate reintegration

Return migrants are often stigmatised in their communities of origin, with return perceived as a failure. This concern must be addressed among return migrants, assisting with reintegration for dependents (school enrolment, assistance in finding housing and accessing local health care) and preparing them for a return to their community. Addressing the families of returnees appears to be an important part of the social support offered for reintegration. More broadly, communication towards the community itself to shift the perception of returnees through support for associations of returnees and information campaigns on return migration can help ease the difficulty.

1.1.19. Supporting the mainstreaming of reintegration of return migrants in national policy can improve available support

Recent years have seen the inclusion of return migrants and of reintegration assistance in policy documents in many origin countries, including Nigeria, Afghanistan, Tunisia and Senegal, for example. This reflects the priority it has assumed for destination countries, the technical support offered to origin countries in developing and drafting these policy documents, and the availability of earmarked resources from donors to address this population. It also reflects the awareness of the specific needs of return migrants. Public services in origin countries have not always been quick to adapt to serve return migrants, even in the presence of a formal commitment. This may be due to a negative perception of return migrants, an assumption that they have their own resources, a misunderstanding of their needs, or a lack of clarity over responsibilities for this group among national services and those serving diasporas and migrants abroad.

One means pursued to reinforce capacity while implementing return assistance is to favour and support the use of public services as part of the reintegration package where possible, through referrals or involving public authorities in case decisions. In addition, it may require raising awareness in public administration of reintegration issues and programmes (training of officials, meetings and workshops) and co-opting of key decision makers. Liaison officers from donor countries can also underline the need to mainstream support for returnees. A clear plan for the transfer of competencies, structures and/or services to the origin country and support the gradual transition of beneficiaries towards use of mainstream services is one means of reinforcing mainstreaming. Nonetheless, returnees are often sceptical of public services and prefer to rely as long as possible on donor-supported services, complicating efforts to mainstream. Managing their expectations remains a challenge, but can be addressed by clear deadlines for files to be transferred and services to be transitioned.

1.1.20. Continuous case management can reduce information gaps and drop-out and improve evaluation

Return and reintegration assistance programmes in host countries attempt to ensure continuous case management, so that the returnee who asks for assistance in the host country has a smooth transition from pre-return preparation to arrival and post-return reintegration. While there is always some drop-out after return, and some returnees do not show up to start their reintegration, most make contact within a few months of return. Ensuring that returnees have a chance prior to return to meet – through video or telephone – their contacts in the home country helps ensure continuity, and most projects integrate this into their procedures.

Monitoring and evaluation are only as reliable as the information which underpin them. In the programmes reviewed, most of the information is provided by operators and implementers themselves, since they are in regular contact with the beneficiaries. Registering service provision, reporting on resource allocation and providing assessments on outcomes are part of the tasks of operators, although these are usually in addition to their main activities.

1.1.21. Data sharing platforms are important

Data sharing is essential in this process, not only for case management, but also for monitoring and evaluation. This is often lacking, due to privacy concerns and the difficulty of sharing information across partners. Transnational case management is sometimes conducted by the same agency, but generally involves some transfer of responsibility for the case to an implementer and partners providing the assistance. In order to deal with this, platforms have been developed for sharing data. One system which allow multiple partners to access basic information according to needs, respects individual anonymity and can host different kinds of reintegration programmes is RIAT, developed by the Belgian Federal Agency for the Reception of Asylum Seekers (Fedasil) but scalable to other agencies and programmes.

One particularly difficult issue beyond programme data is sharing personal information between origin country and host country authorities. Prior to return, many origin countries have pressed for detailed information on returnees, which can assist in orienting them towards services. Destination countries have been reluctant to share personal information, for protection of the individual from potential negative consequences and to ensure that obstacles to return do not appear. On the other side, origin countries are reluctant to share information on their nationals with other countries after return, even when this is useful for programme monitoring and evaluation. This is a particular issue when public authorities are involved in providing services to returnees within programmes, or co-ordinating their cases, as they may see any obligation to report on their nationals to foreign authorities as a violation of sovereignty.

1.1.22. There is no single definition of sustainable reintegration

To date, no single understanding of "sustainable reintegration" has served as a benchmark for assisted return and reintegration programmes. Working definitions used by countries and actors vary, also according to origin-country circumstances, the migrant involved, and the means, scope and timeline under which many programmes operate.

An absolute reference of self-sufficient and well-being, such as the one developed and promoted by the IOM, is useful to guide intervention but can be difficult to use for programme evaluation. The latter requires taking into account individual characteristics and comparison with non-migrants and return migrants who did not receive support. A definition based exclusively on the baseline of the surrounding community neither takes into account conditions of the individual prior to migration nor the possibility that returning to the status quo is not perceived as a positive outcome.

Even in countries which do not have a formal definition of sustainability, a minimum expectation of reintegration is that it will reduce resort to remigration – specifically, irregular migration or migration out of a lack of acceptable alternatives.

1.1.23. A development perspective requires a different definition of sustainability…

A development perspective assesses sustainability by the extent to which reintegration support contributes to the development of the origin country. In addition to expecting the individual returnee to benefit, as above, it extends to consider overall impact – economically, politically and socially. Programmes are sustainable when there is a net economic benefit for the origin country; when the political leadership shares the goals of the programme and integrates them into legislation and administrative practice; when the programme contributes to societal acceptance of return migrants.

1.1.24. …which includes care not to create different forms of inequalities

One of the risks identified in reintegration programmes is the creation of inequalities. Inequalities reflect differences in what is offered to migrants and what is offered to non-migrants, as well as the quality gap between state or public structures and those created or funded by donors. A further risk is to accentuate the inequalities already associated with migration, such as between regions which receive high levels of return migrant investment and those which do not.

Reintegration programmes which go beyond individual support address these risks primarily by ensuring that non-migrants have access to structures and services created; this is the approach taken by GIZ, for example, in its Advice Centres in countries of origin. Another means is to reinforce the capacity of the public sector to provide services to all residents, including returning migrants. By ensuring that support structures have an exit strategy to wind down their activities and transfer competences, the risk of in inequality of service is reduced.

The wide variety of origin-country contexts means that the capacity building process is at different points in each country and policy domain. In less developed countries, where social and employment support structures are weak, the inequality in service promises to persist for a long time, especially if the services offered through reintegration assistance are high level. In other countries of origin, working with local public institutions or strong civil society actors is more immediately feasible and allows to envisage an earlier transfer without sacrificing sustainability.

1.1.25. Sustainability from the host country perspective goes beyond the outcome for the individual to that of the programme…

Support for reintegration from host countries responds to different kinds of expectations. First, that returns through the programme are less expensive than forced return. Removal is a more costly undertaking than voluntary departure. In addition to shifting from removal to voluntary return, cost savings also come when the programme leads to more or faster returns than would otherwise be the case, involving migrants who would not otherwise return. Another savings is to facilitate return of migrants whose stay is costly reducing the expenditures related to reception and support in the destination country. Costly stay can include for example persons with health needs which could nonetheless be satisfactorily met in the home country, or persons who represent social cases such as those living precariously or at risk for delinquency.

Second, that return is effective: at a minimum, recipients of reintegration assistance are not expected to return except through legal channels. The programme cannot be a pull factor for irregular migration or, within Europe, attract applicants from other European countries.

1.1.26. … and the policy as a whole

Sustainability also reflects policy goals beyond the individuals involved in reintegration assistance. It represents a necessary counteroffer to forced return in a political debate, supporting the legitimacy of an asylum system which contemplates dignified return and tempering potential controversy attracted by forced returns. For countries signatory to the Global Compact on Migration, it responds to Objective 21, which includes reference to reintegration.

A reintegration programme can also contribute to improved relations with origin countries, addressing concerns over the impact of returns by providing assistance. Several host countries explicitly refer to the possibility of additional support being related to cooperation in the sphere of migration management, including readmission cooperation.

1.1.27. Evaluation of reintegration programmes is complex and partial

In light of the multitude of objectives and the different expectations in terms of sustainability, the current evaluation framework appears in most case inadequate to fully measure the sustainability of reintegration assistance programmes. In the absence of a normative or common definition of sustainability, all programmes consider the number of participants and evaluate their outcomes in terms of remigration, outcome of the reintegration plan (such as income generating activity) and often self-reported well-being. The number of returning migrants and how they fare after return are indeed important indicators but are not sufficient for evaluation of programmes, since such programmes respond to many more objectives.

From a development perspective, evaluation of sustainability must take into account the impact on return migrants (as above), but also the impact on the community as a whole. Some indicators are already sketched out in existing evaluation objectives, such as the impact on non-migrants, local and family level perception of return migrants, or political support for mainstreaming reintegration assistance and the incorporation of reference to return migrants in policy frameworks and strategies and inclusion in administrative guidelines. While the latter are easy to measure, indicators requiring surveys are more costly and rarely undertaken. Longitudinal surveys, involving a local comparison group, are, a prerequisite for establishing a baseline for comparing returnees with non-migrants and assessing the long-term impact of programmes on individuals while accounting for their characteristics. The IOM framework is a basic for collecting multiple data points and can contribute to the comparative assessment.

A further complication in evaluating individual outcomes is the cost and complexity of follow-up, especially beyond the horizon of assistance. The non-response rate – the disappearance of beneficiaries – is frequently an issue even within the short timeframe of assistance. Tracking down returnees, and administering a longitudinal survey, is costly and difficult. Data on remigration is extremely rare.

Finally, it is difficult to disentangle the impact of programmes on return numbers and individual outcomes from other factors. Return decisions are largely motivated by considerations outside the programme – including the political and economic context in the origin country, the difficulty of remaining in the host country, the risk of forced removal, and individual characteristics.

1.1.28. Positive individual outcomes of reintegration assistance are not in themselves an indicator of programme sustainability

Reintegration assistance aims to support a positive outcome, although the definition varies among donors and categories of beneficiaries. Receiving assistance improves the situation of returnees relative to those returnees who do not receive assistance, but this in itself is not enough to justify the expense. The success of reintegration – as positive as it may be for the individual returnee – should be considered in other terms: its contribution to bolster the ability of host countries to offer alternatives to forced return to other potential beneficiaries (programme credibility); the destigmatisation of return in local communities (improved environment for all returning migrants); and the capacity of origin country institutions to include returnees in mainstream services.

1.1.29. Evaluation should expand to better capture financial sustainability and the impact on origin country institutional and social capacity to support reintegration

While one argument for promoting assisted return and reintegration is that it is less expensive than alternatives, each return is an individual case and represents its own savings. Little attention is given in most programmes to the cost of non-return or the cost of removal relative to individual cases of return assistance. While it is difficult to capture the role that assistance played in the return decision, it is often possible, based on nationality and other characteristics, to assess how difficult and costly it would have been to remove the same returnee. Some programmes take this into account in discretionary allocation of additional assistance. Few programme evaluations, however, take into account the costs savings of returns based on individual characteristics. Notably, persons from countries to which removal is not possible due to difficulties in obtaining travel documents, or those who are likely to spend long periods in detention, represent larger cost savings than persons for whom removal is straightforward and rapid. Social service cases and health cases both represent a larger burden for taxpayers; their return is a larger savings. Fedasil in Belgium for example considers the cost of six months treatment as a benchmark for resources it can invest in organising an assisted return of health cases. The ability to estimate and report on cost savings represented by returns can be a powerful tool to better target programmes and justify higher expenditures for complex cases.

A related question is the difference between cash and in-kind assistance. The shift to the latter has not been accompanied by an evaluation of outcomes. Indeed, if programmes are exclusively designed to provide an incentive to accept return, cash appears to be a simpler and more effective incentive, and certainly preferred by migrants considering return. In contrast, in-kind assistance brings additional benefits and responds to other objectives of programmes. However, a rigorous comparison on outcomes has not yet been conducted.

Evaluation in the future also needs to refer to alternative solutions, to account for whether objectives assigned to programmes can be met more effectively through other policy measures. Increasing the number of returns, for example, might be better addressed through enforcement and compliance efforts outside the scope of reintegration assistance. Voluntary return is effective in accelerating issuance of travel documents and facilitating return, but cooperation of origin countries may also be obtained through diplomatic measures and liaison activities. Increasing the capacity of origin countries to support the reintegration of return migrants may also be achieved through development cooperation, including support to actors serving the population in the origin country. Reintegration assistance does not occur in isolation.

1.1.30. National approaches remain distinct, but some interventions can be mutualised

National approaches remain very distinct, reflecting differences in institutional arrangements and the composition of the target groups. Many good practices seem nevertheless transferable. More importantly, there are a number of practices which are already mutualised and which can be further expanded. In particular, fee-for-service reintegration assistance programmes can share implementers and apply common standards, and use the same data sharing platforms and monitoring and evaluation surveys. Community-based evaluation of reintegration can benefit from mutualisation, as it allows for cost savings but more importantly the opportunity to conduct external evaluations rather than rely on internal project monitoring, and to reach beyond the horizon of individual support measures. More coordination with origin countries on policy change and information provision would lead to greater coherence and effectiveness. Cross-referral of beneficiaries can allow for greater coverage of support and information programmes aimed at the resident population and targeting return migrants, particularly those who did not make contact with programme providers prior to return.

In the medium term, however, the multitude of objectives, the differences in resources available and the varying expectations in terms of monitoring suggest that mutualised programmes will coexist alongside national and even regional or grassroots led channels of support for returnees. Likewise, individual reintegration assistance packages designed to provide an incentive for individuals to accept assisted return will continue to exist alongside community-based interventions in the origin country addressing the context for reintegration. Improved co-ordination among these interventions is possible – at the level of national representation in the origin country. Liaison officers at diplomatic missions can strengthen the ties among different programmes. A stronger role should also be taken at the EU level to ensure that different programmes work more closely together.

> **Box 1.2.** Summary of the main recommendations to improve the sustainability of reintegration programmes
>
> **Increase the visibility of opportunities for assisted return and reintegration**
> - Better target potential return migrants with information campaigns and messaging about the options for reintegration support, including through social media
> - Identify key moments for communication about options for return and reintegration assistance. For asylum seekers, this includes the moment of communication of final refusal.
> - Focus on appropriate locations and contexts (set and setting) for promoting return to potential beneficiaries and their communities
>
> **Invest in reinforcing the legitimacy of return as an acceptable outcome to a migration project**
> - Partner with trusted actors in the destination and origin country, notably civil society organisations, community leaders and caseworkers
> - Work with public and non-governmental stakeholders to improve consensus around circumstances where return is a potentially positive option
> - Shift from information provision to support for developing a reintegration plan and a vision of life after return
> - Support initiatives which address the stigmatisation and negative perception of return in communities of origin
>
> **Adapt reintegration assistance to both individual needs and the cost-savings represented**
> - Strengthen psychosocial support in the reintegration process before and after return
> - Focus in-kind packages on the support needed, including broader family needs, rather than the amount of funding available
> - Allow greater expenditure for complex cases, taking into consideration potential costs associated with the difficulty of removal
> - Balance scope and ambition of programmes against the number of potential beneficiaries targeted or applying
>
> **Improve coordination and referral**
> - Ensure continuous case management from the destination to the origin country

- Include pre-return training opportunities where possible to reinforce skills for return and maintain motivation
- Strengthen communication, referral and exchange among implementers of individual and community initiatives to support reintegration, through visits and liaison activities
- Invest in shared platforms for case management, data exchange, monitoring and evaluation, building on existing models

Invest in the capacity of origin countries to support reintegration and maximise development impact

- Open initiatives in the origin country to embrace and serve all return migrants and potentially also local residents
- Ensure that individual reintegration assistance is compatible with and contributes to existing reintegration programmes
- Empower communities of origin to develop local solutions and support existing grassroots initiatives benefitting returning migrants

Expand evaluation of programmes

- Expand the use of external monitoring and evaluation beyond project reporting by implementers and partners, including through building the capacity of local expertise
- Measure individual outcomes of returnees against the difficulty of the starting point rather than in absolute terms
- Broaden assessment of individual outcomes beyond the reintegration plan and the timeline of support to include longer-term capacity to adapt
- Ensure that monitoring and evaluation effectively cover different groups of returnees and their households

2 Return migration: scope and drivers

Return migration is difficult to measure, since much of it is spontaneous and goes unrecorded, although official data exist on forced return and voluntary assisted return in most OECD countries. The literature suggests that return decision-making is complex and influenced by a variety of factors including the conditions in the origin and destination country, individual and social factors, and, to a limited degree, policy interventions.

The chapter reviews the terminology used in discussing return migration. It then examines the scope and nature of return migration. It reviews the literature and evidence on the factors leading migrants to decide to return to their country of origin.

2.1. The scope and nature of return migration

Internationally comparable statistical information on return migration is limited. Attempts to measure the phenomenon in a comparable manner face two difficulties: the lack of a shared definition of return migration and the lack of data. Yet, knowing who returns and in what number matters for both the host and the home country, as the characteristics of returnees, in particular their education levels and the length and nature of their stay abroad, affect their probability of return, as well as the sustainability of their reintegration after their return.

Return migration occurs in different ways. The usual distinctions consider whether it is spontaneous, initiated by the migrant and without state involvement, or organised and enforced by state authorities (Box 2.1).

Box 2.1. Key Terminology: Forced, Voluntary and Assisted Voluntary Return

Forced return is "a migratory movement which, although the drivers can be diverse, involves force, compulsion, or coercion." **Voluntary return** is "the assisted or independent return to the country of origin, transit or another country based on the voluntary decision of the returnee." (IOM, 2019[1]).

Voluntary return can be either spontaneous or assisted: **Spontaneous return** is "the voluntary, independent return of a migrant or a group of migrants to their country of origin, usually without the support of States or other international or national assistance." (IOM, 2019[1]). **Assisted voluntary return (AVR)** is the "administrative, logistical, financial and reintegration support to rejected asylum seekers, victims of trafficking in human beings, stranded migrants, qualified nationals and other migrants unable or unwilling to remain in the host country who volunteer to return to their countries of origin" (IOM, 2019[1]).[1]

Assisted return programmes have come to include *reintegration* assistance in addition to *return* assistance. In addition to pre-departure counselling, return and travel assistance, **Assisted Voluntary Return and Reintegration (AVRR)** programmes offer cash and/or in-kind assistance to support re-insertion in their country of origin. Assistance may involve some or all of these: business start-up coaching and counselling, labour market counselling, vocational training – including on-the-job training – internships and job placement, housing, health care and children's education.

In practice, return categories are not always distinct and involve varying degrees of voluntariness among the beneficiaries of both AVR and AVRR programmes (see Newland and Salant (2018[2])). For migrants in an irregular situation or asylum seekers with little chances of obtaining protection, AVRR may be a compelled choice, even in the absence of physical coercion. Some see return as voluntary only when individuals have alternative legal options and can make decisions based on a free and informed choice. As persons in these situations represent an expanding group of beneficiaries of AVRR, the line between forced and assisted voluntary return blurs.

Alternative descriptions have been used by scholars to describe situations where "voluntary return" occurs when options are severely constrained – e.g. "compelled return" (Cassarino, 2008[3]), "nominally voluntary return" (Gibney, 2008[4]) and "soft-deportation" (Leerkes, van Os and Boersema, 2017[5]). Several European countries, for example Austria, Norway and the United Kingdom, use the term "assisted return", instead of 'assisted *voluntary* return', for their programmes.

Data on spontaneous outflows are difficult to capture, unless there is a reporting requirement in the destination and origin country, or a survey in the origin country capturing returns (see Table 2.1). The OECD collects data on reported outflows of the foreign population from selected OECD countries through its Continuous Reporting System on International Migration, which are published in the annual OECD

International Migration Outlook (OECD, 2020[6]). Other approaches look at changes in the stock of foreigners and assume that residual outflows are directed to the origin country, rather than a third country. Regardless of the measure used for outflows, they appear to be significant: an OECD analysis (2008[7]) has found that, depending on the country of destination and the period of time considered, 20% to 50% of immigrants leave within five years after their arrival, either to return home or to move on to a third country (secondary emigration). Migrants who arrive for family or humanitarian motives have a lower return rate than economic migrants.

There is no standardised definition that would allow for comparisons of the size and composition of spontaneous outflows across datasets. There are differences in the geographical references chosen (country of birth, nationality or country of previous residence); the time references (short-term or permanent migration and return, including circular movements; intended return or actual duration); and return motivations (excluding short-term visits or holidays). Further, existing data sources do not allow for random sampling, as there is a lack of appropriate sample frames (population registers, censuses, general surveys). The smaller specific surveys that are available, e.g. the MAFE survey in Senegal, are costly to undertake and are often non-representative as they are collected by directly seeking out returnees, or are selected by areas of high return incidence, which means they are not representative at country level. More generally, the fact that returnees are often a small and widely distributed group within the population affects the quality of analyses based on the data and makes evidence – on which policy decisions can be based – costly and less feasible to collect.

The European Union's TEMPER project is a recent attempt at overcoming the gap in data and better understanding return dynamics, looking at both permanent return and temporary return/circular migration. It looks at return and circulation between certain destination (France, Spain, Germany, Italy and Poland) and origin countries (Senegal, Argentina, Romania and Ukraine). TEMPER aims to create a "Repository of Migration Surveys" (Table 2.1) and combine information in pre-existent immigrant surveys with new survey data collected in origin countries (González et al., 2018[8]), covering profiles, mobility patterns (return and circulation included), legal trajectories, contacts with origin countries, etc., for different types of migration.

Table 2.1. Examples of Specialised Return Surveys

Survey	Return Migration Definition	Sampling	Sample Size
ETF (Armenia, Georgia, Morocco 2011)	Left at 18 years or older, returned no more than 10 years prior	Nationally representative sample of non-migrants + snowball sample of returnees (in non-migrant households or in the neighbourhood)	1 311 return migrants, of which 398 from France, 272 from Spain, 203 from Italy
NOPOOR (Ecuador 2014)	Returned from Spain, lived there for one year or more, returned one year or more	Snow-ball sampling + recruitment workshop + website, leaflets	450 return migrants (out of 1 000 expected)
MAFE (Senegal 2008)	Left for Europe at 18 years or older; born in Senegal and has had Senegalese citizenship	Ares with different return incidence; and a listing operation was carried out in each of the selected survey sites	54 Return migrants; total 1 500 (including non-migrants)
ENAMIR (Colombia 2013)	Born in Colombia, returned with the intention to reside there again	Stratified sampling (geographical regions with high migration rates) in 2 stages	21.093 households (1 876 return migrants from all destinations)
MED-HIMS (Egypt 2013)	Last returned from abroad to the country of origin since 1 January 2000; who were 15 years or older on last return	Stratification to oversample where migration concentrated in some regions	90.012 households surveyed (5 085 return migrants from all destinations)

Source: EU Temper Project.

Return migration is self-selected. For spontaneous returns, the evidence suggests that the return rate changes over the life cycle of migrants, with higher rates for the young and for retirees. Returns by level of education also produce a U-curve; i.e. the return rate is higher at both ends of the education spectrum.

Return migration tends to accentuate the selection that originally motivated migration. Return migration selection tends to be the reverse of the initial selection process for migration: if the host country attracts mainly skilled migrants, return migrants will likely be less skilled on average than the remaining immigrants in the host country, while if the host country attracts relatively unskilled workers, the better skilled among them are most likely to return (Borjas and Bratsberg, 1996[9]). Selection in return must be accounted for in analyses of return and reintegration outcomes, as it can lead to endogeneity problems and produce biased estimates.

Beyond spontaneous returns, destination countries arrange **organised returns** – either through **assisted voluntary return programmes** or through **forced removals**. Coverage of the target population is partial. To monitor return rates, Member States must provide Eurostat with statistics on the enforcement of migration legislation, which means that comparable data on return decisions and executions are available for EU countries. On the aggregate level (EU 28, including the UK until 01 February 2020), orders to leave peaked at more than 533 000 in 2015, a record high since 2011, and have remained at around a half million since, with annual variations. In line with this, returns peaked at 250 000 in 2016, the highest level since 2010, but have been falling steadily since then (Figure 2.1). In 2016, less than half of the migrants ordered to leave the European Union did so. In 2017, just above one third did. This figure is not the actual return rate, since it does not take into account time lags, appeals, spontaneous returns and other resolution of status obviating a return order. The 2017 renewed Action Plan of the European Union (European Commission, 2017[10]) aimed at increasing return rates.

Data trends on organised return vary greatly across EU Member States, due to different policies and enforcement capacities for forced returns, as well as to each country's position in the irregular migration routes – and their evolution over time. Thus, in 2015, almost one in five orders to leave for the EU28 was issued by Greece, which drove the overall increase. Country trends have diverged from the aggregate picture. In Spain, for instance, orders to leave almost doubled in 2018 relative to the 2015 figure, reflecting shifts in irregular migration routes (from Eastern to Western Mediterranean route). In 2015, France issued a lower number of orders to leave than in 2013-14, but the figures have grown steadily ever since.

In the EU, since 2014, Eurostat collects a broader set of data on return, including by type of return (voluntary, forced, other), assistance received by the returnee (assisted, non-assisted return), agreement procedure underlying return, citizenship, and destination country (i.e. country of return). Specifically, it includes data on "third country nationals – ordered to leave; returned following an order to leave; who have left the territory by type of return and citizenship; who have left the territory by type of assistance received and citizenship". However, considering that those data are collected by countries on a voluntary basis, not all data for countries implementing AVR are reported in the Eurostat database. Further, spontaneous departures are usually not tracked.

Recent initiatives on the European level aim at overcoming various gaps in measuring return migration, with a focus on measuring return of migrants falling into categories which are subject to removal. The European Commission is implementing Integrated Return Management Application (IRMA), a secure web-platform for integrating all EU return activities. The restricted information exchange platform connects EU Member and Schengen States, the European Commission, the European Border and Coast Guard Agency (Frontex) and the relevant EU funded programmes at operational, practitioner level to collect data on return and readmission activities.

Other OECD countries also publish statistics on returns. In the United States, figures distinguish forced returns between removals and returns; the latter involves cooperation and does not carry the same re-entry ban. Removals averaged about 370 000 annually over the past decade, with a peak in 2012-13, while returns have fallen sharply, from more than 800 000 in 2008 to 100 000 in 2017. In 2017, about two-thirds of returns were to Mexico and one-fourth to the Northern Triangle (El Salvador, Honduras and Guatemala). 41% of removals were of criminals. Returns were largely to the same destinations, although Asia comprised 20% of returns in 2017. Voluntary departure from the United States – when aliens facing deportation decide not to contest their removal and to leave on their own, rather than have a deportation on their record – have been increasing. Voluntary departure fell from 23 900 in FY2012 to 8 400 in FY2016, but rose again to 23 800 in 2018 (Thompson and Calderón, 2019[11]).

Figure 2.1. Number of third country nationals ordered to leave, persons returned, and the return rate (%) in the European Union, 2008-19

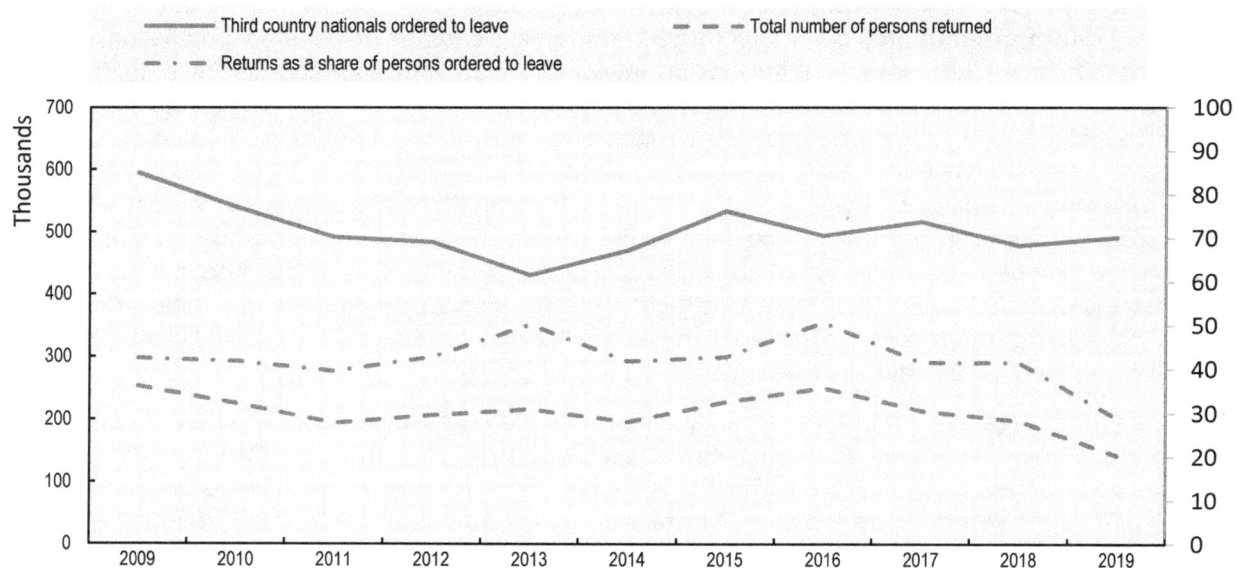

Source: Eurostat, 2019.

Canada distinguishes between forced removals and voluntary compliance with removal orders. Total removals in 2018-19 stood at 9 600, down from 17 500 in 2012 but increasing since the 2016 figure of 7 400. About 60% of removals are forced, with the remainder voluntary, with travel costs borne by the returnee and not by the Canadian authorities. In Japan, annual removals averaged about 350 between FY 2013 and FY 2018; about 10 persons received AVRR annually. In addition, about 6 600 persons subject to removal left on their own without assistance annually. Israel publishes figures on voluntary departures, distinguishing between those returning to their origin country, a resettlement country or a third country. The number of voluntary returns has stood at about 3 000 annually in recent years, although the programme targets Eritreans and Sudanese and most do not return to their origin countries, but rather depart to other destinations. Australia removed about 7 700 refused asylum seekers between 2010 and 2015, comprising about one-third of all asylum seekers with negative decisions over the same period (Cuthbert and Song, 2017[12]). In the past five years, Australia further removed about 6 000 persons.

In addition to governments, implementers and service providers also acquire statistics. IOM, the largest global provider of both AVR and AVRR programmes, collects voluntary return data under its various programmes on a regular basis. IOM data include the number of migrants assisted, migrants' host and origin countries, as well as sex, age and reintegration support. IOM data also include information on assisted migrants by specific vulnerability (namely, unaccompanied and separated migrant children, migrants with health-related needs and victims of trafficking).

Since 2010, IOM publishes these data on its AVRR page and in its publication on "Return and Reintegration: Key Highlights" (IOM, 2019[13]). In 2018, IOM assisted a total of 63 300 migrants through its AVRR programmes worldwide, representing a 12% decrease compared to 2017. Of the migrants assisted, almost half – 30 900 individuals, or 49% of all AVRR beneficiaries – returned from two countries, Germany and Niger, each with about 15 000 return migrants. The other countries sending large numbers of AVRR beneficiaries home included Greece (5 000 migrants), Austria (3 500), Djibouti (3 400), Belgium (2 800), Netherlands (2 100), Morocco (1 500), Turkey (1 500) and Italy (1 000). This reflects that a large part of the return assistance provided through IOM is from non-OECD countries. Over the past years, the figures for assisted return of stranded migrants within Africa has increased. Since January 2018, IOM Libya has assisted more than 17 500 stranded migrants to return to 32 countries across Africa and Asia.

Spontaneous returns are more difficult to measure and the return of naturalised immigrants or even legal permanent residents is generally unrecorded or partial. Precise data are thus largely limited to persons whose return involves state authorities in the destination countries, especially forced returns. For many of these returns, the data available do not go beyond nationality, age and gender. Rarely do these include the duration of stay, the grounds for removal or more detailed individual characteristics. Kosovo, for example, registers repatriated Kosovars in its own Case Management System, with detailed information, but does not capture information on other returns. There remain substantial gaps in the knowledge about who is returning to which countries and in what numbers. Since returnees' characteristics – and their capabilities and vulnerabilities – determine their outcomes upon return, as well as their specific needs for reintegration support, AVRR programmes require better understanding of target group profiles along different return corridors.

2.2. Drivers of return decisions

While there is a well-established literature on how migrants make the decision whether and where to move, and some research on refugee return, there has been less research on the migrant return decision-making process. Most research has been conducted with migrants who have already returned, giving a retrospective picture of what affected a decision to return, but less information on what drives migrants not to return. The literature suggests that return decision-making is complex and influenced by a variety of factors including the conditions in the origin and destination country, individual and social factors, and, to a limited degree policy interventions. Within this literature, much of the evidence is from cases of spontaneous return – i.e. by migrants who were under no obligation to leave the host country or were under no constraint to return.

The main structural reasons assumed to explain migrants' decision to return relate to the situation in the host country, but also to the opportunities open to them in their origin country. Existing studies based on interviews with potential returnees from/to different countries find contradicting results as to whether destination or origin country factors weigh more heavily (Black et al., 2004[14]; Koser and Kuschminder, 2015[15]; Strand et al., 2011[16])):

- *conditions in the destination country*: prospects for a future in the country, failure to integrate into the host country, living conditions, asylum policies, chances of forced return and others.
- *conditions in the origin country*: safety, human rights, political, economic and social, personal relationships and personal resources in the home country (family, housing, job opportunities, networks, ties, debt), etc.

Most existing studies on return migration seek to explain the return of labour migrants or those who migrated irregularly for economic reasons, with different migration theories generating competing hypotheses with regard to the determinants of return (Figure 2.3).

Studies on migrant return have focused on persons who have returned, rather than those who did not choose to return. For most, return is motivated by economic considerations. On the one hand, return of labour migrants is explained as a logical step after migrants have earned sufficient assets and knowledge to invest in their origin country. For example, looking at Turkish migrants who returned from Germany in the 1980s, (Dustmann and Kirchkamp, 2002[17]) propose that the reason why migrants return is that they expect higher returns from self-employment opportunities in their country of origin in the long run. Dustmann and Weiss (2007[18]) make a similar argument looking at migrants in the United Kingdom: migrants return if the human capital acquired in the host country has a higher return at home. Preferences for consumption at home and higher purchasing power in the country of origin are other factors motivating return.

A contrasting strand in the literature associates return migration to the failure to integrate in the destination country. The supposed intention behind migration projects is seen as maximizing utility by migrating to places that allow individuals to be more productive. Thus, if the expected increase in productivity cannot be realised, the individuals are likely to return. For Germany (Constant and Massey (2002[19]) and Canada (Lam, 1994[20]), two studies find that exposure to unemployment in the host country labour market increases the probability of return. For immigrants who find it difficult to join the labour market, however, access to a social security system in the host country can reduce their propensity to return. Reagan and Olsen (2000[21]), Jensen and Pedersen (2007[22]) and Nekby (2006[23]) obtain similar results for the United States, Denmark and Sweden, respectively.

The empirical evidence on return decisions suggests that ultimately, a complex interplay between home- and host-country related reasons motivates return. A large household survey in 11 countries of origin (OECD, 2017[24]), captured more than 3 000 return migrants. They reported their main reason for return (Figure 2.2). The main reason for return was an overall preference for the home country, followed by the failure to obtain legal status in the host country and difficulties in integration.

Figure 2.2. Reported reasons returnees came back to their home country

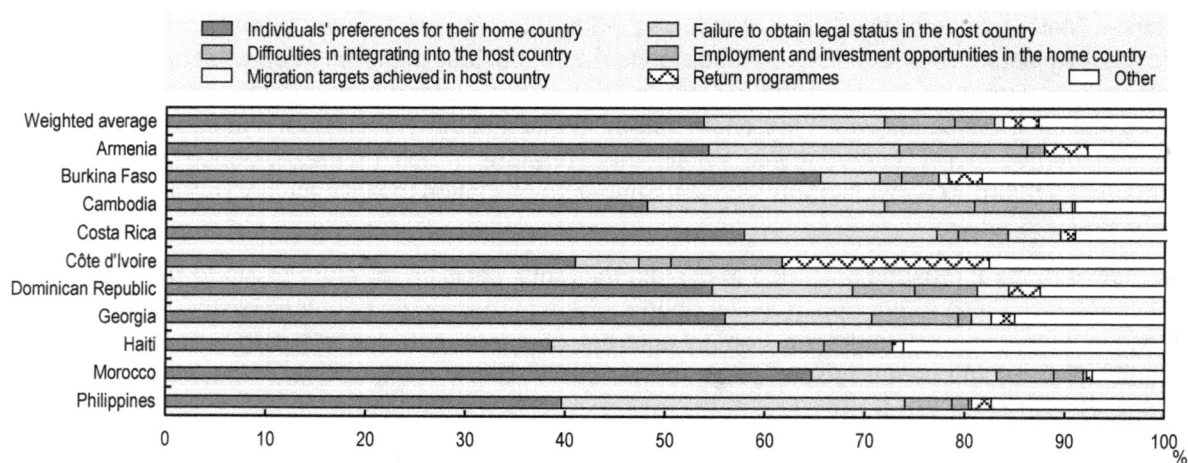

Source: IPPMD survey data. See (OECD, 2017[24]).

De Haas, Fokkema and Fihri (2015[25]) examine return intentions based on survey data of Moroccan migrants across different European countries. The survey indicates that structural integration through labour market participation, education and the maintenance of economic and social ties with receiving countries do not significantly affect return intentions. At the same time, investments in and social ties to Morocco are positively related to return, and socio-cultural integration in destination countries is negatively related to return migration intentions.

Social relations, both in the destination and origin country, are key in migrants' return decision (Flahaux, 2017[26]). In their survey of (potential) return migrants in both destination and origin countries, Koser and Kuschminder (2015[15]) find that changes infamily relations were the most frequently mentioned reason for return. Constant and Massey (2002[19]) find that having a partner in the origin country increases propensity for return for all migrants, whereas having a partner in Europe reduces return probability. The presence of children reduces return probability. Aradhya (2018[27]), for example, finds that immigrant fathers of daughters in Sweden are less likely to return, with the explanation that they expect better opportunities for them in a more gender equal Swedish system. Ultimately, while social relations are a key factor influencing the decision to return, they are largely beyond the scope of policy interventions. A 2014 survey of returnees in Tunisia by the National Institute of Statistics found that the main reasons for return were to accompany family, to return home, but also – for 12% - to get married (OECD, 2018[28]) (Hammouda, 2020[29]).

Figure 2.3. Factors influencing individual return decisions by level

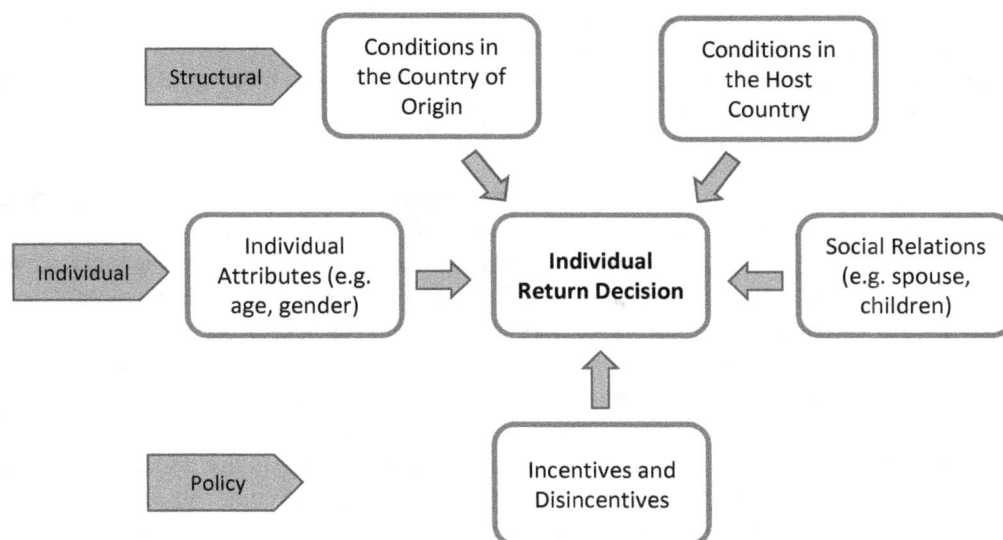

Source: Based on Black et al. (2004).

Several studies show that reasons for initial migration are linked to return (Aydemir and Robinson (2008[30]) in Canada, Klinthäll (2006[31]) in Sweden, Shortland (2006[32]) in New Zealand, Bijwaard (2010[33]) in the Netherlands). Students are the most likely to return while refugees are the least likely, and students and labour migrants return earlier. As expected, work-related factors are more important in predicting return of migrants who left for economic reasons. In comparison with labour and family migrants, return decisions of (rejected) asylum seekers depend more strongly on structural factors in the origin country. For asylum seekers, economic factors are less important than political factors (Black et al., 2004[14]; King, 2000[34]; van Wijk, 2008[35]), although they also have socio-economic reintegration concerns (Klinthall, 2007[36]; Zimmermann, 2012[37]).

These findings have implications for return policy. Unsurprisingly, Brekke (2015[38]) finds that AVR uptake by rejected asylum seekers in Norway is highly dependent on political factors in the origin country, especially in (post-)conflict contexts. In a somewhat similar study, Leerkes et al. (2014[39]), who examine AVR uptake amongst rejected asylum-seekers in the Netherlands, find that voluntary return is less common towards countries with low levels of freedom and/or safety and/or GDP. A recent study of Syrian refugees in Lebanon found that return intentions were contingent on the situation in Syria rather than conditions in Lebanon, including the socio-economic well-being of refugees and their access to services (Alrababa'h, Casalis and Masterson, 2020[40]).

Regarding AVRR more specifically, one question which has been investigated is whether financial incentives – cash payments, in particular, but also reintegration services and support – affect the decision to return voluntarily. The literature suggests that financial incentives alone do not significantly influence potential returnees' decisions. Studies in the French context suggest that most beneficiaries of AVRR had already planned to return, considering the funding as a bonus rather than a decisive factor (Daum, 2002[41]). In Norway, return support appears to be one of the factors contributing to the decision, but not the principal factor (Sønsterudbråten, 2018[42]). A transnational study in the Netherlands and Nigeria underlines that among those who decided to return, the most recurrent reasons are the stress of being undocumented, the family and related 'triggers' that occurred in Nigeria, and the threat of deportation – rather than AVRR (Benhayyoun, 2018[43]). Black et al. (2004[14]) find that most of their respondents believed assistance would in any case not be sufficient to overcome more fundamental obstacles to return – most significantly insecurity and longer-term unemployment. Brekke (2015[38]) finds that "while return and reintegration programs may facilitate and increase the quality of assisted returns, [there is] no clear-cut link to the quantity of such returns". During the global financial crisis of the late 2000s, several OECD countries – Spain, Japan and the Czech Republic – introduced cash payments to unemployed foreign workers as an incentive to return home, even if they held residence permits allowing them to stay. These programmes appeared not to affect the return decision – and indeed, many returned home without taking the incentives when the benefit was tied to a re-entry ban (OECD, 2009[44]).

The role of provision of information and return counselling has received little attention in the literature so far. Nonetheless, there is some evidence that uptake of AVR can be influenced by information from certain credible figures. Leerkes, van Os and Boersema (2017[45]) find that uptake of AVR is highest when "native counsellors" from the migrants' origin community are employed. The use of "native counsellors" was most effective with irregular migrants living outside of state reception facilities who are not engaged in regular return counselling that occurs in the centres. This finding is likely related to higher trust placed in counsellors and the ability to communicate in the origin language. Apart from published studies, different agencies administering AVRR programming also conduct analyses within their programmes, surveying participants about their return decisions. Questions about factors leading to the decision to take assistance are usually included in programme evaluations, both internal and through external evaluators or researchers. For example, an evaluation following up 1 300 participants of a German programme asked about the influence of counselling and the availability of financial assistance on the return decision. For about one-third of respondents, counselling strongly affected their decision, while only one in seven reported that financial aid strongly influenced their decision **Invalid source specified.**. More comparative research on differences in AVR uptake based on different models of return counselling applied in EU destination countries is necessary (Kuschminder, 2017[46]).

Regardless of the information provided, return decisions are the "outcome of a complex mix of migrants' choices and constraints on staying or moving" (van Houte, 2016[47]). The literature on migrants' decision to return voluntarily depicts a complex process largely determined by factors beyond the scope of punctual policy intervention in the destination country, e.g. structural conditions in the country of origin or family relations. The existing evidence suggests that incentives set by AVRR, while they might accelerate return, cannot initiate a decision to return. Many of the factors which are found to affect the return decision have little to do with the incentives, support and conditions offered under the heading of "return and reintegration" policy. These include, for example, likelihood of access to international protection, the prospect of alternatives to protection such as leave to remain for other grounds, the conditions for migrants in an irregular situation, and the likelihood of ending up in removal procedures.

References

Alrababa'h, A., M. Casalis and D. Masterson (2020), *Returning Home? Conditions in Syria, Not Lebanon, Drive the Return Intentions of Syrian Refugees*, Innovations for Poverty Action , Washington D.C.   [40]

Aradhya, S. (2018), *Diversity of Legacy. The Experience of Immigrants and their Descendants in Sweden*, Lund University. [27]

Aydemir, A. and C. Robinson (2008), "Global labour markets, return, and onward migration", *Canadian Journal of Economics*, Vol. 41/4, pp. 1285-1311. [30]

Benhayyoun, S. (2018), *Here no king. There no king. Perceptions of Return among Undocumented Nigerians in the Netherlands and Returnees in Nigeria*, Leiden University, Faculty of Humanities. [43]

Bijwaard, G. (2010), "Immigrant migration dynamics model for the Netherlands", *Journal of Population Economics*, Vol. 23/4, pp. 1213-1247. [33]

Black, R. et al. (2004), *Understanding Voluntary Return*, Home Office Report 50/04. [14]

Borjas, G. and B. Bratsberg (1996), "Who Leaves? The Outmigration of the Foreign-Born", *Review of Economics and Statistics*, Vol. 1/78, pp. 165-176. [9]

Brekke, J. (2015), *Why go back? Assisted return from Norway*, Institute for Social Research, https://www.cmi.no/publications/file/5800-why-go-back-assisted-return-from-norway.pdf. [38]

Cassarino, J. (2008), *Return Migrants to the Maghreb Countries: Reintegration and Development Challenges*. [3]

Constant, A. and D. Massey (2002), "Return Migration by German Guestworkers: Neoclassical versus New Economic Theories", *International Migration*, Vol. 40/4, pp. 5-38. [19]

Cuthbert, N. and J. Song (2017), *Removal of failed asylum seekers in Australia: A comparative perspective*, Lowy Institute for International Policy, Sydney, https://www.lowyinstitute.org/sites/default/files/documents/Removal%20of%20failed%20asylum%20seekers%20in%20Australia.pdf (accessed on 7 August 2020). [12]

Daum, C. (2002), "Aides au "retour volontaire" et réinsertion au Mali : un bilan critique", *Hommes et Migrations*, Vol. 1239/1, pp. 40-48. [41]

de Haas, H., T. Fokkema and M. Fihri (2015), "Return Migration as Failure or Success?: The Determinants of Return Migration Intentions Among Moroccan Migrants in Europe", *Journal of International Migration and Integration*, Vol. 16/2, pp. 415-429. [25]

Dustmann, C. and O. Kirchkamp (2002), "The optimal migration duration and activity choice after re-migration", *Journal of Development Economics*, Vol. 67, pp. 352-372. [17]

Dustmann, C. and Y. Weiss (2007), "Return Migration: Theory and Empirical Evidence from the UK", *British Journal of Industrial Relations*, Vol. 45/2, pp. 236-256. [18]

European Commission (2017), *On a More Effective Return Policy in the European Union - A Renewed Action Plan*, European Commission, Brussels. [10]

Flahaux, M. (2017), "The Role of Migration Policy Changes in Europe for Return Migration to Senegal", *International Migration Review*, Vol. 51/4. [26]

Gibney, M. (2008), "Asylum and the Expansion of Deportation in the United Kingdom", *Government and Opposition*, Vol. 43/2, pp. 146-167. [4]

González, A. et al. (2018), "Preparation of survey tools for merged dataset", *Working Paper Series Temporary versus Permanent Migration*, No. 14, Temper EU Project. [8]

Hammouda, H. (2020), *Retour et Réintegration Durable en Tunisie*, OECD, Paris. [29]

IOM (2019), *2018 Return and Reintegration. Key Highlights.* [13]

IOM (ed.) (2019), *Glossary on Migration.* [1]

Jensen, P. and P. Pedersen (2007), "To Stay or Not to Stay? Out-Migration of Immigrants from Denmark", *International Migration*, Vol. 45/5, pp. 87-113. [22]

King, R. (2000), "Generalizations from the History of Return Migration", in Ghosh, B. (ed.), *Return Migration: Journey of Hope or Despair?*, International Organization for Migration. [34]

Klinthall, M. (2007), "Refugee Return Migration: Return Migration from Sweden to Chile, Iran and Poland 1973 1996", *Journal of Refugee Studies*, Vol. 20/4, pp. 579-598. [36]

Klinthall, M. (2006), "Retirement Return Migration from Sweden", *International Migration*, Vol. 44/2, pp. 153-180. [31]

Koser, K. and K. Kuschminder (2015), *Comparative Research on the Assisted Voluntary Return and Reintegration of Migrants*, International Organization for Migration, Geneva. [15]

Kuschminder, K. (2017), "Taking stock of Assisted Voluntary Return from Europe : decision making, reintegration and sustainable return : time for a paradigm shift", *EUI RSCAS Global Governance Programme*, No. 31, European University Institute. [46]

Lam, K. (1994), "Outmigration of Foreign-Born Members in Canada", *The Canadian Journal of Economics*, Vol. 27/2, p. 352. [20]

Leerkes et al. (2014), *Rejected and departed from the Netherlands? A study into the backgrounds of the variation in assisted voluntary return among rejected asylum seekers*, Wetenschappelijk Onderzoek- en Documentatiecentrum Cahiers 2014–03. [39]

Leerkes, A., R. van Os and E. Boersema (2017), "What drives 'soft deportation'? Understanding the rise in Assisted Voluntary Return among rejected asylum seekers in the Netherlands", *Population, Space and Place*, Vol. 23/8, pp. 1-11. [5]

Leerkes, A., R. van Os and E. Boersema (2017), "What drives 'soft deportation'? Understanding the rise in Assisted Voluntary Return among rejected asylum seekers in the Netherlands", *Population, Space and Place*, Vol. 23/8. [45]

Nekby, L. (2006), "The emigration of immigrants, return vs onward migration: Evidence from Sweden", *Journal of Population Economics*, Vol. 19/2, pp. 197-226. [23]

Newland, K. and B. Salant (2018), "Balancing Acts: Policy Frameworks for Migrant Return and Reintegration", Migration Policy Institute. [2]

OECD (2020), *International Migration Outlook 2020*, OECD Publishing, Paris, https://dx.doi.org/10.1787/ec98f531-en. [6]

OECD (2018), *Talents à l'étranger: Une revue des émigrés tunisiens*, OECD Publishing, https://dx.doi.org/10.1787/9789264308855-fr. [28]

OECD (2017), *Interrelations between Public Policies, Migration and Development*, OECD Publishing, Paris, https://dx.doi.org/10.1787/9789264265615-en. [24]

OECD (2009), *International Migration Outlook 2009*, OECD Publishing, Paris, https://dx.doi.org/10.1787/migr_outlook-2009-en. [44]

OECD (2008), "Return Migration: A New Perspective", in *International Migration Outlook 2008*, OECD Publishing, Paris, https://dx.doi.org/10.1787/migr_outlook-2008-7-en. [7]

Reagan, P. and R. Olsen (2000), "You can go home again: Evidence from longitudinal data", *Demography*, Vol. 37/3, pp. 339-350. [21]

Shortland, P. (2006), *People on the Move: A Study of Migrant Movement Patterns to and from New Zealand*. [32]

Sønsterudbråten, S. (2018), *Fafo-rapport 2018:16 Assistert retur En kunnskapsstatus*, Fafo, Oslo. [42]

Strand, A. et al. (2011), *Between two societies Review of the Information, Return and Reintegration of Iraqi Nationals to Iraq (IRRINI) programme*, CMI Report. [16]

Thompson, C. and A. Calderón (2019), *More Immigrants Are Giving Up and Leaving the U.S. | The Marshall Project*, The Marshall Project, https://www.themarshallproject.org/2019/05/08/more-detained-immigrants-are-giving-up-court-fights-and-leaving-the-u-s (accessed on 7 August 2020). [11]

van Houte, M. (2016), *Return Migration to Afghanistan*, Springer International Publishing, Cham. [47]

van Wijk, J. (2008), *Reaching out to the unknown. Native counselling and the decision making process of irregular migrants and rejected asylum seekers on voluntary return*, International Organization for Migration. [35]

Zimmermann, S. (2012), "Understanding repatriation: refugee perspectives on the importance of safety, reintegration, and hope", *Population, Space and Place*, Vol. 18/1, pp. 45-57. [37]

3 Institutional context of return and reintegration

In the countries covered by this review, recent legislative changes have shifted responsibility for promoting and implementing return and reintegration programmes. In many but not all countries reviewed, migration and development bodies are tasked to work together. More broadly, programmes have a wide variety of partnerships in place. Implementing partners in origin countries range from international organisations to civil society bodies to branches of the destination country institutions.

3.1. Recent changes in legislation and parliamentary debates on return

With policy makers under growing public pressure to manage migration, questions of how, when, and under what conditions irregular immigrants and rejected asylum seekers can be returned to their origin countries received increased political attention in the past years. In several countries covered by the project, regulations have been modified in order to increase the efficiency of return, both voluntary and forced.

In Switzerland, recent policy development was influenced by concern over the possible negative consequences of lengthy asylum procedures. This concern was reflected, for example, by a 2016 "Postulat" to parliament, charging the government to commission a report on the nexus between integration and return. The Postulat was driven by a hypothesis that integration during the asylum process hinders return following a negative decision. The introduction of the new Swiss Asylum System on 1 March 2019 entailed an accelerated asylum procedure. Under this accelerated process, the asylum procedure must be finalised within 100 days, including appeal and deportation where an application is rejected. The revision of the asylum procedure has had implications for when and how voluntary return is promoted in Swiss asylum centres.

Germany, too, has seen several parliamentary requests for information from the government – regarding its return and reintegration activities. The German government passed a set of eight bills on immigration in 2019. The package included the "Orderly Return Law" (Geordnetes-Rückkehr-Gesetz) – which facilitates the return of failed asylum seekers and expands related powers of police and immigration authorities. The new law's aim is to "significantly increase" the proportion of successful deportations.

In 2017, Norway released its second "5-year Return Strategy", developed by the Ministry of Justice and Public Security (MoJ). The current strategy, to run through 2022, stresses the facilitation of rapid and effective returns through readmission agreements, international cooperation and country-specific strategies as the main goal of Norwegian return policy.

In September 2019, Denmark transferred the responsibility of registering asylum seekers from the National Police to the Danish Immigration Service in the Ministry of Immigration and Integration. From August 2020 onwards, a new return agency in the same ministry handles rejected asylum seekers including voluntary return previously also under the mandate of the National Police.

Ensuring that returns of irregularly staying third-country nationals take place effectively, and stepping up the European Union's (EU) return rate has also been a political priority at the European level in recent years, especially since the 2015 peak in arrivals of asylum-seekers and irregular migrants (Box 3.1).

Box 3.1. European Union return policy and legislation

Common rules for managing the return of irregular migrants

The European Union is seeking to harmonise and support national efforts to better manage returns and to facilitate reintegration through common rules on return (the so-called "Return Directive"), agreed by EU States in 2008 and coming into force in 2010. They provide for common standards for the return of migrants without permission to stay, the use of coercive measures, detention and re-entry, while fully respecting the human rights and fundamental freedoms of the persons concerned. The Directive has been transposed into national law by all States bound by it (all EU States except UK and Ireland; plus the four Schengen associated countries: Switzerland, Norway, Iceland and Liechtenstein).

The Return Directive introduced:

- an obligation on EU States to either return irregular migrants or to grant them legal status, thus avoiding situations of "legal limbo"
- promotion of the principle of voluntary departure by establishing a general rule that a "period for voluntary departure" should normally be granted
- a limit on the use of coercive measures in connection with the removal of persons, and ensuring that such measures are not excessive or disproportionate
- providing for an entry ban valid throughout the EU for migrants returned by an EU State
- limiting the use of detention, binding it to the principle of proportionality and establishing minimum safeguards for detainees.

Source: https://ec.europa.eu/home-affairs/what-we-do/policies/irregular-migration-return-policy/return-readmission_en

---

Following prior policy statements, the European Commission identified the effectiveness of EU return policy as a key element in reducing the incentives for irregular migration in its 2015 European Agenda on Migration. Although the Commission has put several initiatives in the area of return forward since the adoption of the agenda, the EU return rate (the number of returns relative to the number of orders to leave the territory of EU countries) has fluctuated. Aiming to increase the rate, the Commission presented a proposal for a targeted revision of the EU Return Directive, the main piece of legislation establishing harmonised standards and procedures to be used by Member States for returning third-country nationals staying irregularly on their territory.

Beyond the increased pressure on facilitating returns, both voluntary and forced, many European OECD countries are increasingly willing to adopt a longer-term approach to returning rejected asylum seekers and irregular migrants, through linking return with reintegration and development assistance. It reduces incentives for re-migration and makes the acceptance of return more likely, both for the migrants concerned and for the origin communities.

3.2. Whole-of-government approach and the institutional location of return

Interdepartmental coordination is an emerging approach in most European countries implementing return and reintegration policies. Some countries have well-developed mechanisms of cooperation: at headquarters and within the partner country. Some countries have made whole-of-government approach a priority but are still working on aligning expectations and establishing cross-government cooperation, although in early stages. In other countries, the whole-of-government approach is subscribed to but has translated into at best limited cooperation in practice.

The governance of return and reintegration policies across OECD countries reviewed within this project is characterised by complex relationships between the various actors involved in coordinating counselling and support from pre- to post- return stages. One important level of coordination was identified between increasingly diverse actors in the administration of the destination country involved in migration policy (Table 3.1). Return policy has implications for various policy areas within destination countries, ranging from domestic policy interests and enforcement of immigration law to international cooperation and development concerns. With development funding shifting towards activities overlapping with migration management, development and foreign affairs have emerged as important actors in the design and delivery of return and reintegration policies.

Table 3.1. Agencies involved in assisted return and reintegration policy

Country	Interior	Development Agency	Justice	Foreign Affairs	Other
Belgium	Migration Office for Forced Returns	ENABEL, the Belgian development agency			Fedasil, Federal Agency for the reception of asylum seekers, under the Ministry for Social Affairs, Public Health and Asylum & Migration
Denmark				The Ambassador-at-large for Migration, under the Ministry of Foreign Affairs of Denmark	Ministry of Immigration and Integration
France	French Office for Immigration and Integration (OFII)				
Germany	Ministry of Interior, Community and Building; Federal Office for Migration and Refugees, BAMF	Federal Ministry of Economic Cooperation and Development; GIZ development agency		Foreign Office, Auswärtiges Amt	
Norway				Norwegian Directorate of Immigration (UDI) ; Norwegian National Immigration Police	
Sweden			Swedish Migration Agency and Swedish Border Police		
Switzerland			Federal Department for Justice and Police, Swiss Secretariat for Migration (SEM)	Swiss Agency for Development and Cooperation (SDC)	
United Kingdom	Home Office	Department for International Development (DFID)	Ministry of Justice (MoJ)	Foreign and Commonwealth Office (FCO)	

Source: OECD Policy Questionnaire on Return and Reintegration 2020.

In several countries, interdepartmental cooperation has been evolving as a result of top-down political pressure for cooperation, particularly against the background of a rise in asylum requests in a number of European countries. Among the countries studied, Germany and Switzerland are the two countries where the cooperation between the development and interior sides are comparatively advanced. Within the Swiss

Federal Administration, the "whole-of-government" approach and interdepartmental coordination are emphasised strongly – including matters of return and reintegration, acknowledging its cross-cutting nature. At headquarters, the Swiss Inter-Ministerial Cooperation (IMZ) Structure constitutes the main coordination instrument between the State Secretariat for Migration (SEM) and the Swiss Agency for Development and Cooperation (SCD). Within the partner country, interdepartmental coordination is coordinated through the Embassy of Switzerland.

In 2015, the German government announced a "coherent approach" to migration policy, involving both development and home affairs actors in response to a spike in arrivals of persons seeking international protection. Since then, all relevant federal Ministries and the Chancellery meet on a regular basis to discuss and coordinate cooperation with partner countries in the area of migration. The area of return and reintegration is no exception to the renewed focus on "whole-of-government" approaches in migration-related work. The Interior and Development Ministries jointly cover the spectrum of pre-return support and reintegration assistance, with the Federal Ministry of Interior, Community and Building focusing on return counselling and supporting voluntary return and fostering the sustainable reintegration of returnees in the respective partner countries, which is achieved together with the work of the Federal Ministry of Economic Cooperation and Development which also focuses on the development perspective.

In both these cases, successful coordination seemed to hinge upon strong commitment at the political level, which goes hand in hand with concrete working -evel mechanisms such as joint commissions and regular working groups. The involvement of different actors can, however, also lead to conflicting policy priorities. Interior ministries and justice departments charged with immigration enforcement may stress return and the rule of law, cost-effectiveness and prevention of revolving-door phenomena, while development cooperation emphasises the developmental effects for the returning migrant as well as for their origin country and community. Home affairs and migration agencies also target different groups than they would without the development side involved in return and reintegration programming. Similarly, there are differences in methodology, as the individual approach of migration management goes counter to the logic with which development assistance functions.

Another difficulty experienced in countries where development and home affairs actors coordinate is related to a certain stigma that migration management-related work carries among many development actors. For one, development actors might be unfamiliar with the range of activities of migration agencies, not knowing that many do not only support AVR, but also have (or seek to have) a much more holistic approach. In the practical area of recruitment, development cooperation staff may be reluctant to work on return and reintegration of persons subject to removal. One example of a response is the effort by Germany's Federal Ministry for Cooperation and Development (BMZ) to discuss and explain why the development side is engaging in return and reintegration, especially towards civil society: on one hand to the part of the public committed to integration and on the other hand to development NGOs. The effort involved awareness raising and information campaigns on the approach, organised jointly with BAMF and IOM. Finally, there are potential frictions at the political level regarding concern over development cooperation becoming a political bargaining chip to obtain cooperation on migration management with origin countries.

In other countries, such as the United Kingdom, the whole-of government approach is strongly emphasised but still in its early stages. The UK Home Office is working with the Foreign and Commonwealth Office (FCO), Department for International Development (DFID) – now integrated into a Foreign, Commonwealth and Development Office (FCDO) – and Ministry of Justice (MoJ) to develop a cross-government approach to reintegration. The Home Office interacts directly with returnees and manages their safe and dignified return, whereas DFID contributed the relevant programmatic experience 'on the ground' to share expertise. The FCDO aims to leverage and increase diplomatic capital by demonstrating the UK's approach to reintegration whil the Ministry of Justice should manage the Foreign National Offender population and are heavily involved with their returns. Concrete mechanisms for cooperation had not yet been established. The situation is similar in Norway, where all return activities are administered under the Norwegian

Directorate for Immigration (UDI). Despite a whole-of-government mandate on return and reintegration evolving on paper, the Norwegian Agency for Development Cooperation (NORAD) is not yet involved in this area in practice.

In France, all return and reintegration activities are exclusively administered on the interior and migration agency side, with no cooperation between migration and development agencies. The responsibility for the voluntary return and reintegration system is situated solely under the French Ministry of the Interior, where all activities are implemented by the French Office for Immigration and Integration (OFII). While the French development agency, the Agence Française de Développement (AfD), has recently acquired a mandate on migration, their work does not cover the return and reintegration issue. In Sweden and Belgium, return and reintegration are also located with the respective migration agencies, the Swedish Migration Agency (SMA) and Fedasil. Until today, Fedasil has only sporadically cooperated through select reintegration projects with their development counterparts, the Belgian Development Agency ENABEL.

Forced return and removal is generally kept at arms length or thematically and institutionally distant from the bodies responsible for promoting and managing assisted return and offering reintegration support. This distance is important for the credibility of services – the ability of potential returnees to receive information on return without risking removal. In some cases, especially in reception and reporting centres, the two functions coexist under the same roof, with efforts to distinguish between the two. The return decision, however, is strongly influenced by the prospect of forced return. The thematic separation of the two policy environments is functional for the operation of return assistance, although coordination at the strategy level may help better inform the target group on the prospects of removal.

One of the consequences of separation is that persons who accept to return can refuse return right up to the moment they are boarding a plane for the origin country. At this point, they are generally transferred to the authorities responsible for removal; most countries will not reconsider their request for later voluntary return without exceptional circumstances. Similarly, persons in removal may also request voluntary return, although a deadline for decision may be imposed before the returnee is tracked for removal or has their eligibility reduced or withdrawn.

3.3. Partnerships in return and reintegration programmes

Many AVRR programmes have come to interlink pre-departure and post-arrival support and reintegration assistance. Such a transnational approach to return and reintegration can only work in cooperation among key actors along the continuum of support. Several publications to guide policy makers and practitioners in the design and implementation of AVRR state the need for engagement and capacity-building of key stakeholders, while calling for stronger mechanisms for coordination.

As AVR is increasingly complemented with support for the reintegration of returnees in their countries of origin, there is increasing demand for cooperation between different political actors in destination countries. Many European destination countries stress the importance of whole-of-government approaches and interdepartmental cooperation. This often involves several parts of the administration, including the development, interior, justice and foreign affairs side. In practice, the coordination among these actors may be complicated by conflicting priorities, especially between domestic political demands and development policy principles (Biehler and Meier, 2019[1]).

Beyond cooperation within destination country administrations – the Whole of Government approach discussed above – international coordination among destination countries is increasing, notably among European countries. ERRIN is one platform that offers opportunities for knowledge exchange and coordination of approaches. It enhances programme coordination to maximise access for beneficiaries from different European countries, and currently leads an initiative to link beneficiaries of reintegration assistance to existing development initiatives. Similarly, the Return Expert Group of the European

Migration Network (EMN) provides a platform for practical cooperation between Member States, bringing together key stakeholders from administrations to share good practices and develop common standards and guidelines for an integrated European approach.

European return policy is a legislative area in transformation: among recent developments are a proposal for a recast of Directive 2008/115/EC (Returns Directive) and a transfer of mandates from ERRIN to the European Border and Coast Guard Agency Frontex (European Parliamentary Research Service, 2019[2]; Council of the European Union, 2019[3]).

The majority of countries work, at least in part, with IOM to implement their AVRR programmes. With over 40 years of experience, IOM has developed into a main actor in implementing AVRR programmes, providing support through individualised counselling and cash or in-kind support upon return. The return assistance provided by IOM has grown beyond Europe to include host countries in Africa, Asia and the Americas. Beneficiaries of the IOM AVRR programmes may include stranded migrants in host or transit countries, irregular migrants, regular migrants, and asylum seekers who decide not to pursue their claims or who are found not to be in need of international protection. IOM in many countries works directly with national and local governments and may partner with civil society organisations, the private sector as well as development assistance bodies, in a wide variety of partnerships.

Civil society organisations, both in destination and origin countries, are a crucial implementing partner of AVRR policies. Most programmes rely on CSOs for implementation of service provision. In some cases, these CSOs have long been engaged in return support and reintegration. CSOs are especially important when dealing with the return of vulnerable groups, particularly unaccompanied and separated migrant children. The European Reintegration Support Organizations (ERSO) network offers a platform to exchange and collect expertise, best practices and information concerning voluntary return and reintegration. It seeks to build up capacities of local organisations working in the field of reintegration and has, in practice, become a platform for service providers.

Many actors are aware that diaspora experiences and insights can help design adequate return and reintegration policies. Policymakers, therefore, engage with the diaspora and incorporate their input when designing return and reintegration policies. In some cases, the diaspora may also help to build trust and obtain access to migrants, in order to better address their concerns regarding possible voluntary return to their country or origin (IOM, 2015[4]). Different diaspora engagement strategies are proposed for destination country agencies designing AVRR programmes, in cooperation with the country of origin (IOM, 2019[5]; Haase and Honerath, 2016[6]). Cooperation with the diaspora is common practice in many European countries' return and reintegration efforts. For example, the German GIZ structures diaspora cooperation in its "Programme Migration and Diaspora", although it also works with diaspora organisations in other programmes. In the United Kingdom, the Home Office liaises with and provides funding to community and faith organisations to advise return and reintegration programmes to their members. Similarly, the Norwegian migration agency (UDI) has a long-term relationship through anonymous "user meetings" addressing all concerns of community members, with the aim of discussing the issue of acquiring credibility with diaspora communities which facilitates mention of return down the line. Often, policy documents on good practices in the economic reintegration of returnees promote cooperation with the private sector. In particular, they recommend private – public partnerships to set up demand-oriented skills' development programmes. The private sector could support reintegration in many ways, e.g. through apprenticeship schemes, on-the-job learning schemes, or mentoring of returnees (IOM, 2019[5]). However, cooperation with the private sector remains sparse and one point which emerged in the study tours is there are few examples of successful partnerships. One reason is the limited formal labour market in many origin countries. However, where destination country firms are active in the economy in the origin country, the possibility is opened for direct relationship with the Chambers of Commerce of businesses of the destination country. Examples of such contacts include the German-Tunisian and German-Kosovo Chambers of Commerce, which have partnered in facilitating the employment of returning migrants with specific skills. Another obstacle raised in the study tours is a negative perception of returnees in general.

Return may bear a stigma, due to associations with possible criminal activity, or due to stereotypes about unrealistic expectations in terms of wage or working conditions.

3.4. Implementing partners and service providers in return and reintegration

In order to ensure that return and reintegration services are effectively delivered to (potential) returnees, most countries work with a broad range of actors as implementing partners – from the return preparation to the reintegration stage. Mapping the different service providers used by different countries from pre-return, return, to reintegration phases helps lay out benefits and potential drawbacks of different partnership approaches. The comparison between different European countries' systems reveals different partnership models and ways to divide tasks and duties between national authorities and implementing partners/service providers (Figure 3.1).

Figure 3.1. Implementing partners in return and reintegration

Destination country authorities work with different types of partners to implement return and reintegration policy

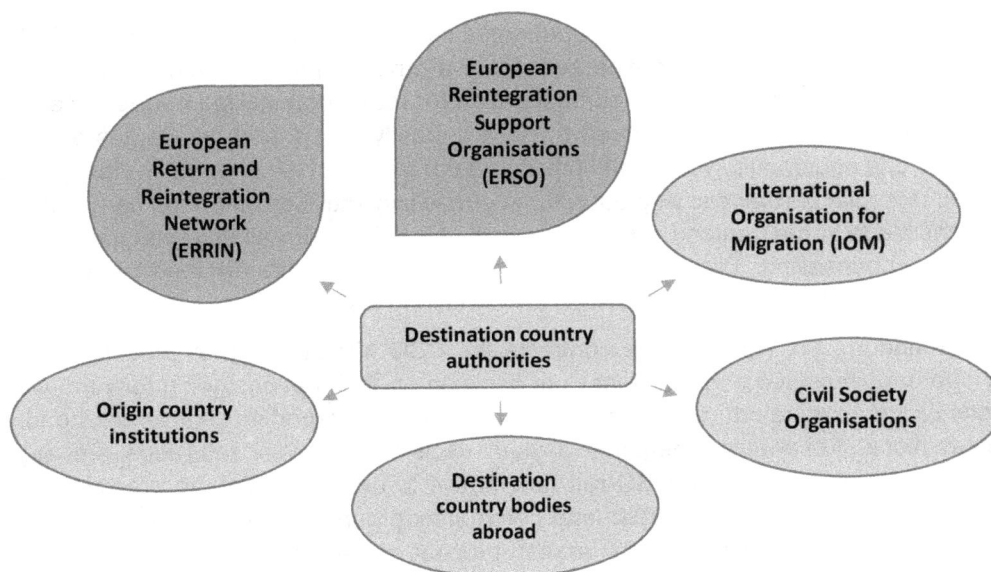

Source: OECD Policy Questionnaire on Return and Reintegration 2020.

Within the project, France was the only country studied which implements its return and reintegration policies entirely through its own authorities, via OFII. In-house counselling by OFII agents is administered in the 31 local OFII offices in France. Reintegration support in the origin country is implemented by OFII country offices abroad, in countries of origin (Morocco, Tunisia, Armenia, Cameroon, Mali and Senegal). OFII in France regularly exchanges with origin countries through an internal information system. OFII contracts service providers for business support in the origin country through regular tenders (every three years). Ideally, OFII seeks to find one service provider to put in charge for support across different geographical regions and sectors. This is not always possible, which means that in practice, OFII works with several service providers of business support per origin region.

In all other countries, the implementation of most aspects of return and reintegration is outsourced to an implementing partner or service provider. Many government authorities in the countries studied mandate large CSOs or international organisations as their return counselling providers or implementing partners, most commonly IOM. Other countries work with a multitude of smaller partner organisations, including

CSOs, private sector organisations and chambers of commerce. In providing reintegration support, some countries partner with national institutions, e.g. employment agencies. As discussed later in this chapter, the choice of implementing partner can have an effect on the populations programmes can reach, how well return migrants' needs are addressed, as well as how programmes are perceived by migrants.

Of the countries studied, Germany has the most complex network of partners delivering return counselling and reintegration support. Due to the federal system, these include both state return counsellors, as well as return counsellors from civil society, frequently funded by the federal states. German federal states each choose actors to implement return counselling. Most state or local authorities cooperate with return counsellors drawn from civil society as well as implementing partners of pre-return qualification measures. Partnerships on the reintegration side are equally diverse, where measures are implemented in close cooperation with political partners in the country of origin – these include ministries in charge of employment promotion and reintegration as well as the related subordinate authorities (e.g. national employment agencies). In countries of origin, training conducted by German authorities is based on enlarging existing programmes of development assistance at community-level, to which they are increasingly adding reintegration components. Partner structures are country-specific and include, beyond political partners, own government agencies (development agency GIZ), CSOs, IOM, as well as private sector organisations (e.g. German chamber of commerce).

The Swiss Secretariat for Migration (SEM) coordinates its Return Counselling Services (RCS) on federal level and trains implementing partners wherever there are new return and reintegration projects in new countries. While the SEM offers financial compensation for return counselling partners, each canton may choose their preferred implementing partner; these are mostly CSOs such as Caritas or the Red Cross, although at least one canton also works with private sector partners. Within most Federal Asylum Centres (FACs), IOM is the main partner carrying out return counselling activities, although cantonal RCS partners may be responsible in some cantons. SEM has mandated IOM to run all its reintegration operations, as well as pre-return counselling. The amount and type of assistance is determined by destination country, and may include a mandate for processes such as monitoring visits.

In the United Kingdom, the Home Office contracts the CSO Migrant Help to provide counselling to all individuals who have received a negative asylum decision on their options going forward, which includes conversations on voluntary return. Government officials working in reporting centres also conduct voluntary return conversations. Following a negative asylum decision, potential returnees are approached by different service providers within the CSO-run "alternative to detention pilots" currently run by the Home Office, testing whether counselling by faith and community groups can provide better outcomes. Return conversations with individuals outside of the asylum process are also held by community leaders engaged to highlight and discuss the possibility of return and options for support. Whilst the Forced Return Service does not have individual return counselling as such, immigration staff embedded within the prison estate have a discussion with foreign national offenders during prison inductions about their return and reintegration and this is ongoing during their time in detention. Return assistance and reintegration support are currently provided by the IOM.

The Norwegian Directorate of Immigration (UDI) regional offices conduct individual return counselling sessions with rejected asylum seekers in Norwegian return centres. For the provision of return counselling, the UDI is assisted by the CSO Norwegian Organisation for Asylum Seekers (NOAS), whose staff provide counselling on both options in asylum process as well as options for assisted return and reintegration support. Each asylum reception centre in the country offers individual return counselling, together with more general information on assisted return and reintegration, by individual staff running these centres. The Norwegian authorities also partner with IOM, who may provide pre-return counselling, and arrange returning migrants' travel back to their origin country. IOM is mandated with implementing the reintegration process and dispensing assistance in the origin country.

In Sweden, a high caseload relative to staff and a lack of partners committed to discussing return mean that potential returnees are offered little pre-return counselling or preparation. There is a "return meeting" after negative asylum decisions on information about benefits and how to get them, which is conducted by officers of the Swedish Migration Agency (SMA) and in some cases by the Swedish Red Cross. SMA officers receive one internal training on return counselling, mostly on technical details (such as re-entry bans and other legal aspects). Police authorities of the Swedish Border Police (SBP) assist the SMA in implementing Assisted Return measures for detained individuals. The Swedish reintegration programme is implemented through the IOM, as well as the ERRIN network for some countries.

The Danish Ministry of Immigration and Integration has contracted out both counselling during the asylum process and return counselling to be handled by the CSO Danish Refugee Council (DRC) under different contracts, with separate mandates and organised independently. There is a daily presence and open counselling by DRC staff at transit and departure centres, as well as early counselling at reception centres around the country. The DRC further provides counselling in prisons and detention centres. Return counselling offers by the DRC are complemented by IOM pre-departure counselling, transportation and post-arrival assistance. Following return, the Ministry of Immigration and Integration provides reintegration support in a range of countries through the ERRIN and ERSO networks (Box 3.2).

Box 3.2. ERRIN and ERSO

Working through the ERRIN and ERSO networks, many European destination countries seek to expand the number of countries in which they can offer reintegration support. Such networks are particularly useful in covering origin countries where there are low return numbers from the destination country, which would not allow to set up bilateral reintegration programmes.

The European Return and Reintegration Network

The European Return and Reintegration Network (ERRIN) is a Member State driven initiative facilitating return and reintegration through joint, operational and innovative solutions, contributing to a common European approach. In addition to offering a favourable financial model (a buy-in fee and 90% of costs covered by the EU), it also has established contacts with implementing partners and worked to promote quality and benefit from scale with partners. When created in the mid-2010s, one possibility which was explored was the full mutualisation of reintegration support through ERRIN; EU Member States participating in ERRIN however maintained their respective programmes and use ERRIN in parallel.

European Reintegration Support Organisations

ERSO is a network of several European Reintegration Support Organisations working closely together in the field of migration and development. The ERSO network's objective is to exchange and collect expertise, best practices and information concerning voluntary return and reintegration. The ERSO network also develops and implements – EU co-financed – joint projects aiming inter alia to enhance reintegration of voluntary returnees and thus the sustainability of the return, as well as to build up capacities of local organisations working in the field of reintegration. For more information, see https://returnnetwork.eu and https://www.ersonetwork.org

---

In Belgium, Fedasil works with two partners, IOM and Caritas, on a split contract. Each is responsible for phases from counselling to reintegration in the origin country. In order to improve programming, Belgian authorities created CONEX, a network linking municipalities and CSOs, with the idea that stakeholders closest to migrants can best determine return assistance needs. The feedback system relies on CONEX partners on the ground – who, for example, identify immigrants of certain nationalities in precarious situations – to provide a signal to Fedasil return desks, who then liaise with their AVRR implementing partners Caritas and IOM to mandate a specific return and reintegration programme addressing the needs of the communities concerned. Then, Fedasil provides funding and information to municipalities and CSOs to inform on the newly created projects. In addition to this continuous loop between municipalities, CSOs, Fedasil and IOM or Caritas in the destination country, CONEX seeks to create a network in origin countries to adequately address the reintegration needs identified by CONEX partners, e.g. assist migrants with alcohol issues by referring them to rehabilitation programmes in origin countries.

The choice of implementing partners and the partnership model has implications for return and reintegration programmes. For one, it might affect the quality of services. There are potential drawbacks to working with only one large organisation, which might lack expertise in working with different populations, or not have the reach and experience with vulnerable populations that a specialised organisation could provide. At the same time, the need to coordinate among several partners makes decision making more costly in a multi-partner environment. The greater demand for coordination requires a corresponding investment in project management but also quality control and individual case management.

Multiple partners, and large projects, make it more difficult to ensure quality control. As noted, among the countries reviewed in the project, German authorities rely on the most diverse network of partners. This is in part related to the distribution of competences, and the patchwork of institutions and partners may yield some variation in standards and practices (Rietig and Günnewig, 2020[7]). To contribute to shared standards, the German Federal Office for Migration and Refugees (BAMF) published a guideline for federal return counselling on its website, which it recommends as guidance for different implementing partners. The guidelines should be complemented by a practical tool in the near future.

Capacity building efforts for implementing partners are also a means to extend quality standards. Through Integplan, the German development agency GIZ organises origin country-specific trainings for return counsellors to establish a better understanding for specific needs of the target group and available offers and referral systems in countries of origin. Fedasil also organises an annual conference of implementing partners to share practices and standards. The European Commission is considering the development of quality standards for implementing partners in origin countries.

To coordinate among implementing partners, data exchange is essential; this is particularly true across international boundaries and when different partners have different needs – case management, monitoring and evaluation. To address this, Fedasil has developed a tool, RIAT (Box 3.3). RIAT provides feedback on cases and allows an overview of caseloads, but is not designed for monitoring and evaluation.

Coordination of in-kind benefits requires payment of fees to the implementing partner responsible for coordination, but this cost does not appear very elevated. In the countries covered, the overhead for managing in-kind support paid to implementing partners or for administering referred cases was not particularly onerous. In Belgium, for example, it was 15% of the reintegration grants (ranging between EUR 150 and 400). In France, the OFII programme pays a fee of up to EUR 1 300 (EUR 720 in the case of programmes implemented with ERRIN partners). GIZ imposes a fee of 14% on cases it manages. This is not much higher than the fees charged for disbursal in cash programmes: in Sweden, the cash establishment support carries a 7% fee. In the projects covered, the fee to implementing partners is in addition to programme costs, which include the entire counselling, referral and data management systems described.

Box 3.3. Transition to Reintegration Assistance Tool (RIAT)

The Transition to Reintegration Assistance Tool (RIAT) is a protocol for case management and monitoring first developed by the Belgian Federal Agency for the Reception of Asylum Seekers (Fedasil).

RIAT is a data-collection and management tool to simplify coordination of different systems among partners and across borders. It was developed to address the lack of an information storage and sharing platform between actors in the host and origin country, to guide case management, and to provide feedback on individual and programme outcomes. From an initial short standard questionnaire meant to offer a low cost and rapid method for data collection providing instant feedback on the return stage of the migration cycle, it has developed into a platform.

RIAT collects information using different standard set of data that has to be collected at certain points in order to ensure good case management. "Key moments" include pre-departure (established when the returnee is first registered as a potential returnee), one month post-arrival (when the reintegration project is drawn up), and at the end of the reintegration project (usually the conclusion of support falls between six and 12 months post-arrival). Data is divided into four levels: operational case handling (the case file), the socio-economic profile of the returnee (interview), returnee experience (interview), and feedback by the caseworker. The return counselling service in the host country thus receives feedback on counselling results and the decisions taken with the origin country service provider following return.

Data collection and exchange occurs at four levels. There is a case file, containing operational case handling information. The service provider inputs information on the reintegration process, based on a short interview with the partner in the origin country. Additional questions on the return experience are also asked as a short module. Further, the service provider in the origin country adds information on the individual return process and reintegration case. The RIAT database includes an indication of vulnerability assessed by the return counsellor and a self-assessment by the returnee. Data access – the ability to see cases and different information – depends on the user role, the organisation and country and the project.

RIAT provides feedback from partners in the origin country to reach the case workers in the host country on specific cases, which allows for better evaluation of services provided prior to return and a better understanding of the outcomes of individual returns of migrants. At the same time, it collects general data on programme outcomes. Since data is provided by partners, it is an entirely internal feedback mechanism, relying on the capacity of case workers to assess situations and provide useful information – especially when fields are qualitative.

RIAT is a platform which can be used by multiple partners in host and return countries, and allows flexibility to include further fields; documents can also be uploaded. The ERRIN harmonisation group has helped make RIAT available to ERRIN members. For the countries funding reintegration services, RIAT provides information on services provided and individual outcomes. For origin country service providers, it allows a single platform for reporting to multiple partners. For ERRIN, the goal is to use RIAT to streamline procedures and data collection, to become the primary tool for managing service contracts. RIAT is designed to support all case management, in national programs and projects beyond ERRIN.

References

Biehler, N. and A. Meier (2019), "Rückkehr und Reintegration. Rückkehrförderung zwischen innenpolitischen Ansprüchen und entwicklungspolitischen Grundsätzen", *SWP-Aktuell 2019/A 50*, Stiftung Wissenschaft und Politik.   [1]

Council of the European Union (2019), *Frontex Programming Document 2020-2022*.   [3]

European Parliamentary Research Service (2019), "Recasting the Return Directive", *EU Legislation in Progress*, European Parliament.   [2]

Haase, M. and P. Honerath (2016), *Return Migration and Reintegration Policies. A primer*, Deutsche Gesellschaft für Internationale Zusammenarbeit.   [6]

IOM (2019), *Reintegration Handbook: Practical guidance on the design, implement ation and monitoring of reintegration assistance*, International Organization for Migration, Geneva.   [5]

IOM (2015), *Reintegration: Effective approaches*, International Organization for Migration.   [4]

Rietig, V. and M. Günnewig (2020), *Deutsche Rückkehrpolitik und Abschiebungen: Zehn Wege aus der Dauerkrise (German return policy and deportations: Ten ways out of the permanent crisis)*, DGAP (Deutsche Gesellschaft für Auswärtige Politik), Berlin, https://dgap.org/sites/default/files/article_pdfs/dgap-analyse-2020-03-de_0.pdf (accessed on 29 September 2020).   [7]

4 Promoting voluntary return

Reintegration assistance is usually targeted at certain groups and eligibility conditional on characteristics of the returnee, including nationality, status and individual circumstances. The return packages considered in this review include a mix of cash and in-kind services, with the latter representing the bulk of assistance. In addition to tailoring packages to the potential beneficiaries, outreach is essential. Counselling migrants is also important to increase take-up, improve pre-return preparation and ensure that the programme matches individual needs.

4.1. Groups targeted with voluntary return assistance

Generally, voluntary return programmes target those migrant populations who have no legal right to stay, or a low possibility of obtaining such right, particularly where their prolonged presence presents considerable financial or social costs for the destination country. In practice, assisted return programmes studied in this project differed in the categories of migrants they target, ranging from a specific focus on rejected asylum seekers, a wider focus on all irregular migrants, to eligibility of permanent residents or recognised refugees who seek assistance in returning to their origin countries.

Most countries do not have clear estimates of their target group, i.e. of the number of potential beneficiaries of AVRR programmes. Depending on the categories targeted with AVRR, however, it might be possible to arrive at an approximate: where the target group of AVRR beneficiaries is limited to (rejected) asylum seekers, the number can relatively easily be construed based on available data on lodged asylum requests and rejected requests in particular (number of asylum applications, number of rejected asylum applications, and number of return decisions). The annual number in this category exceeds 200 000 in Europe, for example (Figure 4.1). Reliable statistics on stocks or flows of irregular migrants, on the other hand, are generally not available.

Figure 4.1. Number of asylum applications and rejections in the EU28

The number of asylum applications and rejections can provide an indication of AVRR programmes' target group size

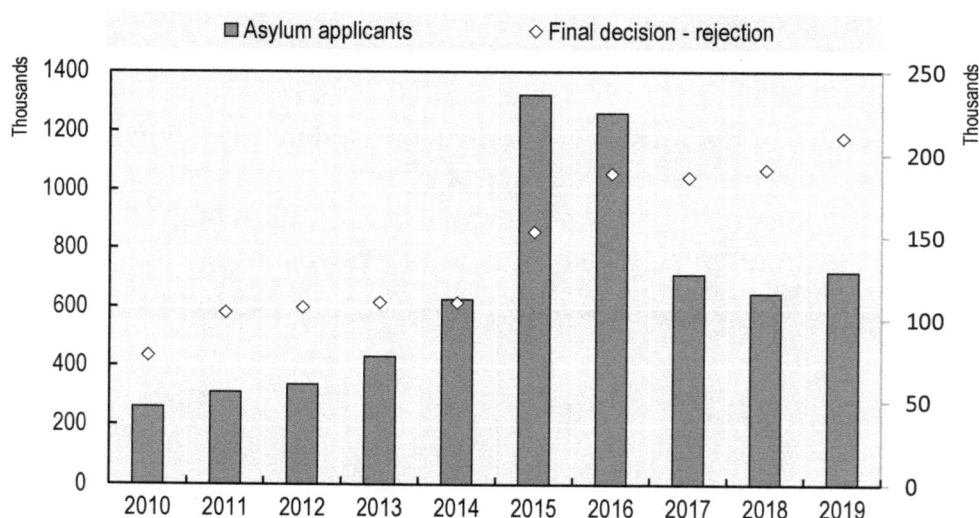

Note: EU28 data on asylum and first time asylum applicants; final decisions on applications (rejected).
Source: Eurostat.

In all countries studied, the main focus of AVRR programmes was on asylum seekers – both during the procedure, at the point of rejection, and after final negative decision. Following the high increase in asylum applications over the past years, the number of rejected asylum seekers has, in turn, also significantly increased. As a result, many European OECD countries have emphasised the need to link the return policy to the asylum procedure as a priority action in this regard, targeting individuals during the asylum procedure, at the point of rejection, and once rejected. Sweden was the only country studied where target group of the AVRR programme were limited to asylum seekers who decide not to pursue their claims or who are found not to be in need of international protection. Switzerland also recognised refugees.

Programmes in Belgium, Germany, and Norway are designed to include migrants in an irregular situation who have never applied for asylum. Germany is the only country of those considered in the study that widens its eligibility criteria for AVRR to migrants with residence permits who seek support to return to their origin countries. Apart from the groups mentioned before, some programmes also address stranded migrants in transit to another country (e.g. migrants in Belgium or France transiting to the United Kingdom). Finally, many countries offer specialised AVRR assistance to migrants in vulnerable situations, such as victims of trafficking, unaccompanied and separated children, or migrants with health-related needs. Programmes must be tailored to meet these groups specific needs that stand in the way of return. The main vulnerabilities in programmes are victims of trafficking, primarily women trafficked for sexual exploitation.

The experience with AVRR over the past years has shown that while categories formally remain the same, the target group may nevertheless be in flux. After the increase in asylum applications in 2015-16 voluntary return went up, but decreased after the surge. Those returns that were more easily facilitated made up the majority of this surge. After those returns, target population of assisted return programmes was made up of those individuals that are hard to reach, avoid authorities, or have special needs (such as trafficking victims, medical cases etc.). Similarly, the composition of countries of origin might change, meaning that the target population consists of those with more structural issues impeding return, i.e. obstacles that are much harder to address through AVRR programmes. AVRR programming must be aware of and adapt to these changes in composition of target group.

One of the main justifications for offering return and reintegration packages in many countries is, as noted, a cost savings over removal or continued stay of migrants ordered to leave the country. Yet, in most countries, criteria for eligibility and magnitude of assistance are only broadly adjusted to the cost of non-compliance. Nationals of countries not subject to a visa requirement, for example, are generally excluded from most benefits, to prevent these from acting as a pull factor when migration costs are low.

Benefit packages are largely standardised without reference to the relative cost of non-departure or forced return. In practice, each case represents a different cost. Some cases may represent a high cost for the host country. For example, migrants subject to removal but who cannot be removed without cooperation in identification and obtaining a travel document are a costly category: detention may last a long time or they may be released. The country of origin may be recalcitrant and refuse to issue documents without the cooperation of the returnee, or pose other obstacles, making forced return impossible. Persons with expensive medical needs may also represent costly cases. On the other hand, forced return may be relatively simple for other groups.

Some degree of discretion in the level of support is available in most countries for cases of vulnerability. In Belgium in particular, for example, the amount to be spent on support for health cases is benchmarked to the cost of six months care in Belgium. This amount may be much higher than the standard package of reintegration assistance but is considered a costs savings. Belgium also grants some discretion in offering assistance to other vulnerable cases, such as persons living on the street.

Less discretion is the magnitude of the reintegration package available in cases of refusal to cooperate in obtaining travel documents, in part to avoid providing an incentive not to cooperate. In the European countries involved in the study, when the origin country refuses to provide documents to the cooperating migrant, other solutions – including regularisation of status – may be considered.

To the extent that returns with assistance are a costs-savings, there are several benchmarks to consider. For persons subject to forced return, the cost of forced return – including personnel costs, public opinion and relations with the origin country – is a key reference. For persons for whom forced return is impossible, and high costs associated with remaining, more margin to increase the package may be useful. As noted, the amount of the package does not seem to be the main factor in return decisions, but no evaluations have focused specifically on groups who are not facing prospect of forced return. A more targeted reintegration assistance package would address the relative costs represented by different categories of potential returnees.

A further issue for targeting is that some beneficiaries may not be priority for return but may reinforce nonetheless the legitimacy of return and the broader sustainability of the return system. For example, OFII in France has a mandate to assist the return of persons with an order to leave the territory. However, its support is also available to spontaneous returnees, including persons with a regular residence permit, such as international students concluding their studies. For this group, OFII can participate in a return project such as entrepreneurial activity, even providing cofounding along with other sources of capital. Support for this category of returnees is not about reducing the pool of persons obligated to return, but about changing the perception of returnees, expanding the network of contacts in the origin country and building goodwill.

4.2. Return packages: in-cash assistance at the point of departure/after arrival

As discussed before, the target groups of the voluntary return programmes are primarily for migrants who wish or need to return home, but require support to do so. In order to provide the means necessary to organise a return, an important pillar of return assistance are financial return packages that cover expenses during travel and immediately after arrival (Table 4.1). The eligibility criteria for return support, which includes transportation costs and cash benefits, vary significantly across countries. Generally, the group of beneficiaries is regulated based on nationality (often excluding countries with visa-free regime for entering the EU), legal status (migrants with residency, irregular migrants, rejected asylum seekers, refugees), type of return (forced returns are often excluded) and personal situation/vulnerability (victims of trafficking, medical cases).

Table 4.1. Eligibility for flight costs and cash assistance

Country	Migrants without permission to stay	Migrants with permission to stay	Asylum seekers, pending claim	Asylum seekers, rejected application	Refugees & those with subsidiary protection	Comments
Belgium	Yes	No	Yes	Yes	No	
Denmark						
France	Yes	No	No	Yes	No	
Germany	Yes	Yes	Yes	Yes	Yes	
Norway	Yes	No	Yes	Yes	No	
Sweden	No	No	Yes	Yes	No	
Switzerland	No	No	Yes	Yes	Yes	
United Kingdom	Yes	No	Yes	Yes	No	Only administrative support (flight cost)

Source: OECD Policy Questionnaire on Return and Reintegration 2020.

In the United Kingdom, all individuals without lawful status are eligible for flight-only support via the Voluntary Return Services (VRS). Individuals who fall into one of the following three groups are eligible for cash/in-kind assistance of the maximum amounts: those who are deemed vulnerable (GBP 1 000), those who are/have been in the asylum process and their family members. Victims of modern slavery (including EEA/EU nationals) can gain return support as a vulnerable individual through VRS. The Home Office is currently looking at increasing eligibility and support for reintegration. Foreign National Offenders who have received a custodial sentence of up to four years (and occasionally beyond four years with exceptional agreement of the Director or by using Senior Manager discretion), can receive GBP 1 500 (if time serving) or GBP 750 (if time served) as well as in-kind support provided via IOM.

In Norway, asylum seekers with a pending asylum claim, rejected asylum application or appeal or a withdrawn asylum application, and those falling under Dublin regulations seeking to return to their home country, as well as any migrant not registered with the government of Norway and without a legal permission to stay in Norway are eligible for voluntary return assistance packages. Any migrants in Norway for purposes other than asylum (e.g. student, family reunification), citizen of any EU, EEC or visa-free country are ineligible. There is exceptional support for anyone assessed as being in a vulnerable situation, mostly victims of trafficking and unaccompanied minors. Any of the above categories who are in country where ERRIN operates will receive reintegration in-kind support.

In France, return assistance covers foreign nationals with at least six months presence in the country, including persons with an order to leave French territory (OQTF) as well as irregular migrants without such an order. France further includes students and young professionals among eligible groups for AVRR, although they are not eligible for the countries that are covered by ERRIN (and URA2 in Kosovo). Germany offers assistance through REAG (Reintegration and Emigration Program for Asylum-Seekers in Germany) / GARP (Government Assisted Repatriation Program), a longstanding programme offering repatriation assistance and a cash benefit. REAG/GARP assistance amounts offered depend on nationality. If a person is eligible for REAG/GARP and application for voluntary return is made no later than two months after asylum application has been decided, individuals are eligible for an additional, one-off payment of EUR 500 in cash.

Other countries adapt the eligibility and/or the amount of support in order to set incentives for cooperation in a similar manner. A new decelerating benefits model was developed in Switzerland with the intention to increase, or at least speed up, assisted return uptake. Under the new approach, the longer an individual is in Switzerland, the less money they are entitled to for assisted return. A different, but similar approach is taken in Denmark, where migrants who refuse to consider voluntary return are moved into the "uncooperative track", after which they are no longer eligible for return assistance. Similarly, Denmark temporarily introduced a time-limited specific intervention for Iranians, offering a higher amount in the first three months of programme; after this, Iranians only received a lower amount.

Table 4.2. Cash return assistance in selected countries

Country	Cash assistance
Belgium	EUR 250
Denmark	
France	650 EUR per person for third countries subjected to a visa requirement. EUR 300 per person for third countries which do not require visa + Kosovo
Germany	Amount of cash benefits available through REAG/GARP return assistance varies by nationality; EUR 1 000 per adult; up to 3 500 per family; possibility of additional assistance for medical needs.
Norway	The IOM Vulnerable Groups Programme offers NOK 8 000 in cash
Sweden	3000 EUR per person or EUR 7 500 per family
Switzerland	CHF 1 000 for adults (CHF 500 for minors). Gradual (declining) approach in the reception centres (reduced in two steps to CHF 500 and 250).
United Kingdom	Up to 50% of the reintegration assistance can be in cash if required.

Source OECD Policy Questionnaire on Return and Reintegration 2020.

Among the programmes examined in the study tours, an open question was whether financial support incentivises the decision to return voluntarily at all, and if so, which amount is decisive. The evidence on the effect of financial benefits on return is inconclusive. Reflecting findings regarding the determinants of return, counsellors working with potential returnees held that financial incentives alone do not significantly influence return decisions, suggesting that most beneficiaries of AVRR had already planned to return, considering the funding as a bonus rather than a decisive factor. However, this observation needs to account for the characteristics of the informant and the moment in which the question is posed. In reporting on the reasons for the return decision, for example, asylum seekers, even after a final refusal of their claim, may be reluctant to attribute influence to the financial offer, since this may undermine the legitimacy of the asylum request. Nonetheless, even follow-up surveys of returnees in the origin country, who have less need to sustain the narrative underpinning their prior asylum claim show that reintegration support – cash or in-kind – was not the main factor in the return decision.

Countries have different approaches to set the ceilings for monetary return assistance. Denmark, for example, like most countries, does so in comparison with the assistance offers in other European countries. The UK currently seeks to determine the appropriate amount through target groups with potential beneficiaries. Feedback from beneficiaries, regardless of the amount of assistance provided, is generally that it is not enough. An important question for many actors devising return and reintegration programmes is setting the adequate amount of assistance in the first place.

A key consideration in setting the amount is preventing financial benefits from creating pull factors, incentivising migration in the first place. To this end, several countries exclude certain nationalities, those with visa-free regimes to Schengen in particular. Further, countries have monitoring systems allowing them to swiftly respond to potential spikes in assistance requests from particular countries. That said, most countries that do monitor for fraudulent activities find that this is an extremely marginal phenomenon. There is no evidence that reintegration assistance is an incentive for others in the origin-country community to migrate in the hopes of obtaining a similar package; just as the assistance is not the main factor in return, other considerations are much more influential in driving migration choices. It does not appear that returnees receiving assistance are in visibly better economic circumstances than they were prior to departure as to induce others to migrate. Indeed, reintegration assistance in many cases may appear to the community only enough to restore the returning migrant to a pre-migration status: for example, resuming a business activity sold to finance migration.

The shift towards in-kind rather than cash occurred in many European countries, although cash is sometimes used alongside or in alternative to in-kind services. A number of factors explain this shift. Cash can be politically more difficult to justify (Swan, 2017[1]), and it is consequently politically more compelling to publicise success stories when positive outcomes are related to in-kind services rather than cash grants. Swan (2017[1]) also notes that cash is not appropriate to "manufacture" a return decision – i.e. to pressure potential returnees into returning, but rather to accelerate return: in the Australian case, it led to a short-term uptick in recourse to return, but created no long standing increase in uptake.

No evaluations comparing the relative effectiveness of cash compared to in-kind assistance have been conducted, including on uptake of return and reintegration assistance, but a number of factors argue for the shift.

First, in-kind services require – but also promote – involvement of more partners, providing funds to implementers and building support for the programmes in participating civil society. Similarly, they may be a response to pressure at the international level to offer such services through intergovernmental agencies. Stakeholder support is increased as more actors are involved. In-kind support can contribute to capacity building in origin countries as well.

Cash may be seen as putting the returnee at risk from criminals or corrupt officials, if it is known that returnees have large sums with them at return, or will receive cash transfers in the following months. Cash transfers are less expensive than managing an in-kind programme, but may nonetheless come with high administrative fees, especially if a partner is required to disburse the sums following return once or more over a certain period. IOM, for example, provides this service, but the cost has increased in recent years.

The donor may have a priority in partnering with the returnee to create a sustainable livelihood, and want to ensure that transfers are invested in income-generating activities, rather than used to pay off debts, provide largesse to family and community, or support consumption. In-kind assistance also implies ongoing contact and relationships and allows for more opportunities for monitoring, evaluation and reporting.

Cash-based programmes may be more appropriate than in-kind services in certain circumstances, especially when the main objective is to secure cooperation from individuals who cannot be otherwise removed, where no partnerships are in place in the origin country to support reintegration assistance. This is the case for Israel, for example, which offers a USD 3 500 grant to eligible applicants (illegal border crossers who have applied for asylum) from Sudan, Eritrea, Ivory Coast, Ethiopia as well as from other countries that do not have diplomatic relations with Israel. Cash may also be effective in accelerating return decisions, especially when available only for a short window of time, as was offered by Denmark to Iranians as mentioned above.

Uptake of assisted return and reintegration assistance is hard to assess within countries and to compare across the countries reviewed in this project. As noted, eligibility for reintegration assistance may be limited for some nationalities who receive return assistance. Table 4.3 reports the number of beneficiaries of different forms or return and reintegration assistance in countries participating in the review. For some countries, only assisted return figures are available. The share of voluntary returns and assisted returns who receive reintegration assistance varies. In Denmark, for example, about 70% of the voluntary departures in 2018 applied for reintegration assistance. In France, the figure was closer to one in four. In Germany, returning migrants receiving return assistance from REAG/GARP have different eligibility levels for post-return reintegration support. Further, for many countries in Table 4.3, reintegration support may also be applied for following return, and these beneficiaries are not included here.

Table 4.3. Uptake of assisted return and reintegration support varies over time and across countries

Beneficiaries of different forms of return and reintegration assistance, 2015-2019

	2015	2016	2017	2018	2019	Note
France	667	1152	1899	2642	1554	Return Migrants receiving Reintegration Support
France	4758	4774	7114	10676		Voluntary Return supported by OFII
Switzerland	548	747	437	309	356	Implemented reintegration projects
Belgium	1631	1974	1607	1486		Return Migrants receiving Reintegration Support
Sweden (Cash)	216	2527	1285	958	482	Return Migrants receiving Reintegration Support
Sweden (In-Kind)		19	621	740	427	Return Migrants receiving Reintegration Support
UK	1645	1353	1562	1968		All assisted returns, with and without reintegration support
Denmark	379	242	362	341		Voluntary departure/return
Norway	1167	1461	571	242	209	Voluntary departure/return
Germany	35514	54069	29587	15941	10201	REAG/GARP Pre-departure assistance

Source: OECD Policy Questionnaire on Return and Reintegration 2020, and evaluation reports.

4.3. Raising awareness of assisted return and reintegration programmes

Outreach activities help to ensure that migrants who may be in need of return and reintegration assistance, as well as other information multipliers such as migrant communities, diaspora and other relevant civil society stakeholders, are aware of AVRR. Fostering awareness of return and reintegration assistance can, in turn, increase the uptake by the target group. There are different ways in which the countries studied in this project promoted information on their return and reintegration programmes. Standard means of communication reached from traditional media such as distribution of leaflets, posters, brochures, billboard advertisement, to information points including a free hotline, a return helpdesk and online websites targeted to people seeking information on voluntary return and reintegration (Table 4.4).

One issue identified in designing outreach measures in the countries involved in the study is that messages are adequately shaped to address identified information needs and are well understood by the target group. Further, since return is a sensitive issue, official messaging needs to be carefully framed to avoid backlash from immigrant communities or the general public. In a context where civil society and diaspora are often hostile to return, some countries have reported negative experiences with more broadly visible general-public campaigns on return, provoking backlash in public opinion. In response to such campaigns, publicly visible campaigns have been reduced, in favour of more targeted channels of reaching the intended public. The German Ministry of Economic Cooperation and Development, for example, started a campaign in 2019 over social media platforms such as Facebook and Google, targeting addressees through tools such as geolocation (identifying foreigners offices within a three-mile radius); tracking use of words such as "refugee" or "reintegration" in search engines to show ads of returnees speaking about their reintegration experience.

Trusted figures are, as noted above (see Section 2.2), influential in return decisions. Concrete examples of using trusted community figures for outreach have been operating for some time. In Belgium, such "native counsellors" are employed by Fedasil to reach migrants in precarious social situations and without legal residence status. In the past, social workers from the same national backgrounds (e.g. Moroccan or Polish, sometimes former homeless or irregular migrants who have become outreach counsellors) have been contracted to build relationships of trust in order to help migrants transition off the streets, connect them with their communities in Belgium, and ultimately to discuss potential return in long-term. Similarly, the UK Home Office works with community liaison representatives to provide counselling. These community liaison officers are not paid, nor are they charged with increasing uptake of return, but they are informed of possibilities for return and reintegration assistance and able to discuss it with potential beneficiaries. A different, but similar effort in trust building are the German "reintegration scouts" who link counsellors and potential returnees to partners in the origin country, which provide knowledge of and connections to the origin community and context and that seek to enhance existing counselling structures provided both by the state and civil society organisations. Some countries take community-based approaches to counselling in the origin country, with information passed to migrants in the host country. The German GIZ, for example, has conducted community counselling for the Ashkali community in Kosovo, discovering that information filters back to Germany and better informs members of the community there. A number of countries, including Germany, conduct specialised networking and awareness raising events.

Table 4.4. Websites informing about assisted return and reintegration offers

Country	Website	Specialised return website?	Languages	Comments
Belgium	www.voluntaryreturn.be	Yes	English, Dutch, Amharic, Chinese, Pashto, Lingala, Serbian, Russian, Ukrainian, French, Albanian, Arabic, Farsi, Mongolian, Spanish, Tigrinya	Website includes both content targeted to potential returnees and people assisting returnees
Denmark	No national website. Information provided by Danish Refugee Council	No	Danish	Website content targeted towards returnees

Country	Website	Specialised return website?	Languages	Comments
France	www.retourvolontaire.fr/	Yes	French, Arabic, Albanian, Dari, Georgian, Urdu, Russian, Bengali, Romanian, English, Portuguese, Armenian, Spanish, Chinese, Pashto, Serbian, Tamil, Créole Haitian	Website content targeted towards returnees
Germany	www.returningfromgermany.de; www.startfinder.de	Yes	German, English, French, Serbian, Albanian, Kosovo, Pashto, Dari Arabic, Farsi, Kurdish	Website includes both content targeted to potential returnees and people assisting returnees
Norway	www.udi.no/en/return/	No	Norwegian, English	Website includes both content targeted to potential returnees and people assisting returnees
Sweden	www.migrationsverket.se/English/Private-individuals/Leaving-Sweden/Rejection-of-application-for-asylum/Returning-voluntarily.html	No	Amharic, Arabic, Armenian, Aerbaijani, Bosnian, Croatian Serbian, Danish, Dari, Northern Sami, English, Spanish, French, Georgian, Icelandic, Chinese, Kurmanji, Meankieli	Website content targeted towards returnees
Switzerland	www.youproject.ch/	Yes	English	Website includes both content targeted to potential returnees and people assisting returnees
United Kingdom	www.gov.uk/return-home-voluntarily	No	English	Website content targeted towards returnees

Source: OECD Secretariat.

Information campaigns have, as noted, moved away from underlining the risk of removal, due to negative perception. Most of the information campaigns focus on building a positive image of post-return integration, although the return decision is motivated by both the perception of opportunities at home and the difficulty of remaining, including the likelihood of forced removal.

In the same vein, reduced support for persons subject to removal – limited allowances, limited mobility, restrictions on employment – are a factor. A hostile environment, as noted, does play a role in return decisions, although no country has an explicitly stated policy to do this. Surveys of participants in return programmes underline the influence of difficult conditions (e.g. (Samuel Hall, 2018[2])). During the 2020 lockdown of the Covid pandemic, some countries saw an uptick in interest in return from persons who were working illegally and unable to meet their basic needs due to the informal labour market – for example, in construction or domestic work – drying up. This group was aware of return possibilities, but uninterested until alternatives became untenable.

In the particular case of asylum seekers, communication is structured by the process and the institutional contacts which occur throughout the process, as well as the setting in which they occur (see Figure 2.1). In principle, communication about return and reintegration occurs throughout the process. Information on voluntary return and reintegration options are provided, in principle, at the start of the asylum process in all countries. However, on the day the asylum request is lodged, most officials note that asylum seekers are not in the right state of mind to hear about return options. Nonetheless, most systems consider it important to inform early in the process and at different steps, to keep the information in the back of the mind of asylum seekers. As the process continues, especially for those who are unlikely to receive protection, the expectation is that they progressively become more amenable to hearing and processing information on possible return options.

Figure 4.2. Stylised "return path" in asylum process

Key phases in return path at which counselling is offered

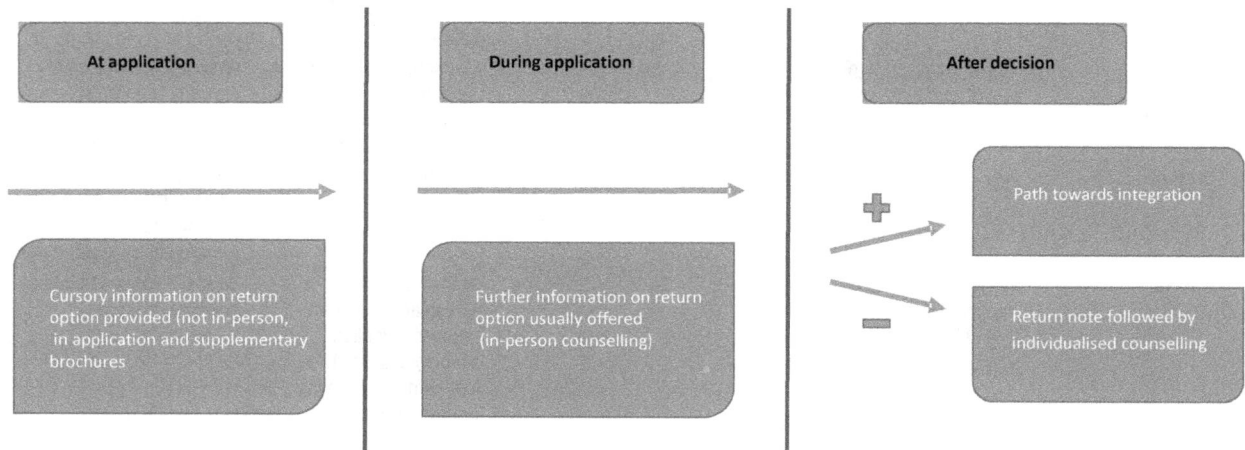

At application — During application — After decision

Cursory information on return option provided (not in-person, in application and supplementary brochures)

Further information on return option usually offered (in-person counselling)

Path towards integration

Return note followed by individualised counselling

Source: OECD Secretariat.

Most return and reintegration systems are set up so that information on the availability of return and reintegration assistance is put in the back of the asylum seekers' mind from the start of the asylum process, even if the asylum seeker does not consider it as an option for themselves yet. The first point of information is usually an information note provided at the point of application for asylum. During asylum interview and individual discussion, counsellors bring up the option of return and reintegration in more detail. Based on the asylum seekers' reaction, these initial contacts determine the right moment to send the person to specialised return counselling services. Often, entities offering return counselling (often IOM or civil society organisations) are physically present in reception centres, providing individual counselling opportunities in on-site offices as well as group presentations.

France was an exception to this model of continuous institutional contact throughout the asylum procedure – in the French system, information on return and reintegration opportunities is provided at the first and last point of institutional contact. OFII agents provide information about return and reintegration to asylum seekers at the point of their application. During the asylum, as well as the appeals process (which can take up to one year), OFII does not interact with individuals. The target group is hard to contact – some are housed in accommodation for asylum seekers, where counselling is not actively provided; others live with acquaintances or relatives; some live on the streets. However, the return counselling process starts as soon as there is a final decision on the asylum case and rejected asylum seekers have received their obligation to leave the French territory (OQTF). On the OQTF paper, relevant OFII addresses and phone numbers are listed and there is information on assistance for voluntary return and return counselling offers.

4.4. Counselling migrants on return and reintegration assistance

Counselling goes beyond provision of information to individually address potential return migrants, ensure they understand their legal situation and options, and potentially to elaborate a vision of return in light of the assistance available. While information provision is passive, even when targeted to specific groups or characteristics of potential return migrants, counselling is interactive. All countries involved in the study tours – indeed, most countries in Europe (European Migration Network, 2019[3])– report having counselling procedures in place, but vary in terms of the extent to which counselling goes beyond provision of information and answering questions to working to bring about a clear understanding of legal obligations and what assisted return would mean for the migrant relative to alternatives.

Generally, the aim of return counselling is twofold: effective implementation of migration policies through compliance with return procedures, and ensuring that potential return migrants gain information about their situation, the different choices and options they have, allowing them to make an informed decision about their future. Making an informed decision about the future means addressing the possibility of return, which can be difficult. One example of this is the Swiss concept, defined as "a change of perspective". Interaction is explicitly aimed at shifting asylum seekers from a presumed "asylum perspective", preoccupied with a negative decision and unable to consider alternatives. The change of perspective is meant to bring them to think of return as an option. The concept considers a mind-set which sustains asylum seekers through often long and uncertain asylum procedures, but which militates against consideration of return. The Swiss approach is shared by many countries. For migrants facing the risk of forced removal, consideration of return may be obscured by anxiety, complicating any effort to discuss return as an option (Olivier-Mensah et al., 2020[4])

4.4.1. Setting of return counselling

Building trust is imperative for counselling, especially where potential returnees have little trust in government-offered assistance. Successful return programmes are able to find the right moment to promote and build trust, in the system, the support offer and the different actors involved. Setting is vital.

Return counselling is best done in a non-directive atmosphere, as well as a safe environment. One means of achieving this is to separate AVRR counsellors from the threat of enforcement. In France, there is no link between return counselling and the police and law enforcement. Seeking counselling is only for information provision – until the person decides to avail themselves of AVRR, they can choose not to provide their details. For OFII, this creates trust, as potential returnees know they are free to leave counselling centres whenever they like. Furthermore, persons who have received an obligation to leave the country, can still use AVRR and may choose voluntary return once they have been apprehended (individuals in detention centres may now also apply for voluntary return). In the Belgian context, return counselling and enforcement are institutionally separate, as Fedasil is not competent on issues of forced return, but solely for assistance for voluntary departure.

Finally, once migrants have made the decision to return, it is not clear whether it is beneficial for them to remain in shared accommodation with other migrants, including (rejected) asylum seekers. For example, Swiss authorities try to let those deciding to avail themselves of return assistance stay in asylum centres, as a way to present the possibility and benefits of return assistance to other inhabitants. In other countries, there is concern that the decision may be reversed due to social pressure. More generally, shared accommodation allows potential beneficiaries to share information about programmes and procedures, comparing the kinds of assistance offered in different origin countries and to different categories of return. This can be an issue when return assistance differs – for example between return under national procedure and under Dublin procedures – distinctions difficult to explain but which can undermine trust and create conflict. Confidential and individual counselling therefore seems a more productive format in these contexts compared to presentations for groups or communities.

4.4.2. Actors involved in return counselling

A number of countries rely on non-institutional actors to provide return counselling, or distance state institutions from direct contact with potential returnees during the counselling process. The location of counselling varies among countries, with an attempt in many to distance return counselling from institutions associated with enforcement.

In Belgium, return counselling is conducted in a separate office, set up as an information space to receive clients. This may involve contracting civil society organisations to participate in return counselling, as Germany does with different CSOs. In the UK, for example, community liaison officers, representing religious or cultural communities, work voluntarily with the Home Office on different issues, and are informed of reintegration assistance programmes so that they can advise those migrants for whom they see return as a positive option and orient them towards the reintegration programme. Recently, Swedish authorities have started to pilot a new means of information transmission specifically for unaccompanied minors, where trusted stakeholders including teachers and accommodation staff can discuss the possibility for return. The Swedish Migration Agency has seen that this can raise trust in their AVRR programmes. In a similar manner, the French authorities aim to open communication channels via service providers that have no link to the OFII, which, as part of the Ministry of Interior, is perceived to have a strong link with (enforced) return by migrants. Such actors include diaspora members, civil society actors (so-called "*associations*").

However, this approach is often complicated by the fact that the stakeholders most trusted by migrants are reluctant to assist in facilitating return and often prefer alternative outcomes to enable migrants to stay in the country. Against this background, the most successful approach to cooperation between authorities and CSOs seems to be based on flexibility in outcomes of counselling, meaning that return is not pushed by all means. For example, Fedasil cooperates with and funds counsellors who work with their target group over longer periods, sometimes for months, before bringing up the possibility of return. While each contact with potential returnees lasts for at least two hours, the counsellor's output in terms of return is low – about 1% overall, although these cases represent a high cost if they remain. Similarly, in Germany, SOLWODI, a CSO supporting vulnerable women, reports that its staff only engages in return for cases where they deem return the most suitable and in the best interest of the migrant, and continue to find options in Germany in all other cases. Thus, cooperation with trusted partners is most successful if they are allowed to continue to push alternative results if that is best for the migrant, aligning return counselling with the civil society organisation or the individual counsellor's self-understanding and convictions.

4.4.3. Topics covered in counselling

Good counselling is not only about providing information about AVRR or guiding through the return procedure itself – it engages the potential returnee and counsellors in conversations where worries and open questions can be shared freely. Often, to begin to imagine life after return, it is necessary to address more general worries occupying a rejected asylum seekers' mind before the individual is ready to discuss a potential return. In order to create a space where this is possible, return counsellors must be impartial in their counselling, have extensive knowledge of the asylum procedure and practices, and possess good conversation techniques and excellent social skills. Some countries train their counselling staff with specific techniques in order to make this possible. Denmark and Norway, for instance, are piloting the "Motivational Interview" method. Acknowledging that rejected asylum seekers may experience apathy and frustration and may have difficulties engaging in conversations about their future, counsellors start off with more general conversations, subsequently encouraging individuals to take smaller decisions regarding their own situation, before bringing up the question of return in later stages. In France, on the other hand, counselling opportunities provided by the OFII are limited to provision of information.

4.4.4. Constructing a vision of post-return life: preparation for return

Trust in the local reintegration partners who facilitate the reintegration support in the countries of origin is important – especially when the programmes only offer in-kind support that is delivered in the country of origin. Trust in the programmes and the local reintegration partners depends among other things on the communication between the rejected asylum seekers and the return counsellors as well as on a good cooperation between the local reintegration partners and the Member States.

Reintegration in the country of origin is a process, which can start already while in exile. For reintegration programmes to be tailored to the individual needs of a returnee, an assessment of the persons' needs, capacities and competencies must be made preferably well in advance of the rejected asylum seekers return. Comprehensive and holistic reintegration programmes are important to ensure dignified and sustainable return.

Counselling sessions with host-country counsellors work on shifting the perception of return in general, but are often unable to help develop a detailed picture of life after return. Contact with persons in the origin country can also help shift the narrative. For example, Denmark offers "go and inform" visits, where origin-country representatives can tell their stories. IOM has representatives in most origin countries who can be contacted to provide potential returnees with information about reintegration opportunities and the context for returnees; a number of countries rely on this possibility to get information. Germany's GIZ employs "reintegration scouts", intermediaries who help public and private actors providing counselling to link with origin country experts who can answer questions and help paint a picture of post-return possibilities for both counselling actors and the target group itself. However, most services acknowledge that counselling cannot necessarily convey realities of post-return life, and try to strike a balance between reassuring the returnee of opportunities to reintegration, while avoiding promising services, assistance or outcomes which are unavailable or unrealistic.

Partners in the origin country regarding the adjustment phase of returnees following return report that even with pre-departure counselling and contacts, many returnees do not fully understand the situation until they actually return. Entrepreneurial projects and expectations of living conditions and reception by families are some of the notions which have to be adjusted after return, even with pre-return preparation.

Counselling is different for certain vulnerable groups. Victims of trafficking are generally referred to specialised services, provided by IOM. Unaccompanied minors are also subject to a separate counselling regime, taking into account the approaching milestone of 18 and the legal consequences. Health cases also require special preparation and are entrusted to specialised support services. Families may also require assistance in preparing return, through pre-enrolment or scholastic orientation for children, to properly time return for continuity of education. Fedasil also addresses the return process for children by providing a workbook in which the child can prepare by assembling a scrapbook of the host country and elaborate expectations of the country of return.

Finally, despite efforts to separate enforcement and voluntary return in the person of the counsellor, and the emphasis on persuasion by providing a positive outlook on return, one can ultimately not deny that the mere threat of forced return is a driving factor in many return counselling conversations. When discussing an individual migrant's options, return is almost always contrasted to the lack of opportunities should the individual decide to stay in the destination country irregularly, as well as the consequences of forced removal.

The possibility of further migration after return may also shift the perception of return, addressing concerns that return will immobilise the returnee in an unsustainable situation (Olivier-Mensah et al., 2020[4]). Persons with secure residence status can experiment with return through visits (such as UNHCR's "go and see" visits) but this is not an option for those in the asylum process or facing removal. The various discussions with return counsellors during visits in project partner countries have shown that re-entry bans set for individuals forcibly removed are often discussed. During counselling, individuals showed great concern for potential bans on future legal entry. In France, there is a two-to three-year ban, the *Interdiction de retour sur le territoire français* (IRTF), for individuals who ignore their OQTF and remains in France. Where a person was forcibly removed from the United Kingdom, they are subject to a mandatory ten year re-entry ban. Depending on the specific reason for the ban, the entry ban ranges from one to ten years, but also includes the possibility of "lifetime ban". One incentive to take up return is the prospect of a reduced visa ban for later return, but there is no guarantee that consular authorities will favourably view future visa applications from persons who previously faced removal, regardless of whether they benefited from AVRR, even when the re-entry ban has expired.

A further issue with counselling is that counsellors may be working against resistance to considering return from other actors also providing advice and support to potential returnees. In Sweden, for example, many of the actors working with asylum seekers sent signals during the asylum process that some solution would be found to stay and integrate; even after a final negative decision, other solutions were proposed to the potential returnee (Lindberg, 2020[5]). The study tours found that a similar ambivalence regarding return was common among actors working with asylum seekers, making counselling more difficult and a shift of perspective harder to foster.

4.4.5. Evaluating the impact of counselling on the return decision

The impact of return counselling on the return decision, and on the outcome of return, is difficult to measure. Some follow-up questions asked to returnees address the role of counselling in the return decision. For example, the German Federal Office for Migration and Refugees conducted a survey of returnees who had received the "StarthilfePlus"cash benefit; among respondents, counselling was reported to strongly influence the return decision in 31% of cases (Schmitt, Bitterwolf and Baraulina, 2019[6]). However, this survey does not cover non-returnees.

Even if there were consistent evaluation, counselling programmes differ greatly in the nature of the intervention. Each potential return migrant is in a different situation, and despite attempts to standardise intervention, the case work approach means that each contact between counsellors and migrants is unique. Outcomes also depend on timing and location; counselling provided to all residents of reception centres, for example, may see a high number of contacts, but while asylum seekers have not received a decision, leads to little uptake of assistance packages. Other counselling services work with people who have contacted them of their own initiative, reflecting an openness to return which predates the counselling itself. The challenge of monitoring outcomes of counselling was also identified by the European Migration Network, which surveyed EU member states and concluded "Most government providers of counselling were interested to measure its impact in terms of increased numbers of effective returns [...] deemed particularly difficult to attain because of difficulties in establishing case-effect relations between counselling and the decision to return" (European Migration Network, 2019[3]).

References

European Migration Network (2019), *Policies and practices on return counselling for migrants in EU Member States and Norway - EMN Inform*, European Migration Network, Brussels, https://ec.europa.eu/home-affairs/sites/homeaffairs/files/00_eu_inform_return_counselling_2019_en.pdf (accessed on 9 August 2020). [3]

Lindberg, H. (2020), *Those who cannot stay: Implementing return policy in Sweden*, DELMI, Stockholm, https://www.delmi.se/en/news/those-who-cannot-stay-implementing-return-policy-in-sweden (accessed on 11 August 2020). [5]

Olivier-Mensah, C. et al. (2020), *Developing Lifeworld Oriented Perspectives for Return Migration: Needs, Vulnerabilities and Support of Refugees in Germany*. [4]

Samuel Hall (2018), *Supporting post-return interventions in Afghanistan-GIZ's Programme for Migration and Development (PME)*.

[2]

Schmitt, M., M. Bitterwolf and T. Baraulina (2019), *Geforderte Rückkehr aus Deutschland: Motive und Reintegration. Eine Begleitstudie zum Bundesprogramm StarthilfePlus (Forced return from Germany: Motives and reintegration. Study accompanying the federal program StarthilfePlus)*, Bundesamt für Migration und Flüchtlinge (BAMF), https://www.bamf.de/SharedDocs/Anlagen/DE/Forschung/Forschungsberichte/fb34-evaluation-starthilfeplus.pdf (accessed on 7 August 2020).

[6]

Swan, G. (2017), *Strengthening Australia's assisted voluntary return program*, Lowy Institute for International Policy, Sydney.

[1]

5 Supporting sustainable reintegration

While the definition of sustainable return and reintegration varies among the countries involved in the project, all require that the reintegration project lead to a positive outcome for the migrant. Packages offer a range of support to meet this goal. Economic reintegration is a central component for most beneficiaries, with business creation the usual project. Training prior to and after return are also included in the package. Reintegration also means settling back into the home community, which may not be fully welcoming, requiring outreach to families and community leaders in the origin country.

A commitment to facilitate safe and dignified return and readmission, as well as sustainable reintegration, has been reiterated under the 2018 Global Compact for Safe, Regular, and Orderly Migration.[1] In particular, Objective 21 of the Compact includes a commitment "to create conducive conditions for personal safety, economic empowerment, inclusion and social cohesion in communities, in order to ensure that reintegration of migrants upon return to their countries of origin is sustainable".

While most actors involved in AVRR programming stress the concept of "sustainable" return as the main desired outcome, there is no common definition of what "sustainability" means in this context. The lack of definitions and established indicators for measurement makes comparisons across studies difficult. A common understanding requires reconciling different perspectives on sustainability. In other words, should the programme lead to a result which is sustainable for the state administering return and reintegration, the origin countries and communities, or the individual returning migrants themselves.

From a migration management perspective, a possible definition of sustainability of return is that people remain in their country of origin and do not re-emigrate. The European Migration Network (EMN), for example, states that: "Sustainable return is return which deters new irregular migration of the returnee and – where possible – of other third country nationals in the Country of Return by consolidating the position of returnees in their home countries and – where possible – enabling the returnee to consolidate the position of other people in his / her community or country of return" (European Migration Network, 2016[1]).

Under this definition, unsustainable return refers to returnees who do not aim to reintegrate and are able to re-migrate irregularly, either back to the previous destination country or elsewhere. Somewhat paradoxically, this definition considers "sustainable" the return of those who are unable to re-migrate, regardless of whether they are successfully reintegrated in their origin country. Defining return purely as the absence of remigration is therefore not without critics. Strand et al. (2016[2]) and Kuschminder (2017[3]) stress that returnees can be "unsustainably returned" when they are not successfully reintegrated, but lack the ability to re-migrate. When re-migration aspiration and ability are distinguished, "sustainable reintegration" cannot be defined simply looking at whether a returnee re-migrates.

Reflecting the inadequacy of using remigration as a proxy for sustainable return, (IOM, 2017[4]) defines sustainable reintegration as:

(a) returnees reaching levels of economic self-sufficiency, social stability within their communities, and psychosocial wellbeing that allow them to cope with (re)migration drivers.

(b) the ability of returnees to make further migration decisions as a matter of choice, rather than necessity.

Reintegration, therefore, is sustainable when an individual is successfully reintegrated in the everyday life, the labour market and the social environment of their origin country and has the resilience to deal with the forces that initially drove their migration. This definition also emphasises that continued mobility after an initial return – including circular migration and the adoption of a "transnational" lifestyle – may in some cases be more "sustainable" than a one-time definitive return to the returnees' place of origin (Graviano and Darbellay, 2019[5]).

The IOM approach, as other definitions in the literature, acknowledges that reintegration is a multi-dimensional process and aims at ensuring returnees' economic, social and psychosocial wellbeing in their origin country. The economic dimension, including employment, income sources, debt, ownership of land or house, is seen as the core of reintegration. The most comprehensive definitions of "sustainable" reintegration go beyond the generation of income. They include a socio-cultural dimension as reflected by networks, participation in local events, self-perception of personal life, membership in organisations upon return. It also requires attention to the safety and security, i.e. perceived safety, trust in the government, access to justice, experienced personal harassment since return (Koser and Kuschminder, 2015[6]). Increasingly, different actors call for consideration of a political and legal dimension to "sustainable" reintegration, including access to anti-discrimination remedies and full enjoyment of civil and human rights (Gesellschaft für Internationale Zusammenarbeit (GIZ), 2018[7])

In addition, some authors suggest that definitions of sustainable return should capture both **objective and subjective dimensions** to sustainable reintegration. Koser and Kuschminder (2015[6]) define return as sustainable when "the individual has reintegrated into the economic, social and cultural processes of the country of origin and feels that they are in an environment of safety and security upon return". This definition focuses on returnees' own perceptions regarding their situation, accounting for the fact that ultimately, returnees' perceived situation determines their re-migration decisions. Recent research explores the importance of return migrants' subjective well-being, life satisfaction and sense of belonging, as well as their re-migration intentions (Lenoël, Şerban and Vandenbunder, 2018[8])

A possible measure of returnees' objective situation is the post-return status compared to pre-migration status. However, as their pre-migration conditions caused them to migrate in the first place, this hardly reflects sustainable return. Another objective measure might be a comparison of the returnees' circumstances with those of the local population. However, it is unclear which segment of the local population would be most appropriate for comparison. Further, the local population may lack access to basic services and safety might be limited for all, providing few opportunities for sustainable reintegration. Indeed, the local population might be in a situation of poverty, instability and stress, which is unsustainable for both non-returnees and returnees by the above definitions.

Sustainable reintegration must therefore be a **multi-level concept**, since "sustainability of reintegration is not only dependent on the returning individual, but also on the local community and the structural situation of the environment of return" (IOM, 2017[4]). When communities perceive return positively, it allows the migrant to return without the risk of being stigmatised, enabling them to re-establish social ties, and facilitating re-insertion into society. This is more likely when return migration positively influences – rather than worsens – conditions in the community of return. Sustainable reintegration therefore has an **individual** level, i.e. the specific needs of beneficiaries and households; a **community** level, i.e. specific needs and concerns of families and communities; and a **structural** level, i.e. access to basic services and safety for returnees and non-migrant populations alike (IOM, 2017[4]).

Table 5.1. Elements and potential measures of the sustainability of return

	Physical	Socio-economic	Political-security
Subjective perception of returnee	(Lack of) desire to re-emigrate	Perceived socio-economic status	Perception of safety, security threats
Objective conditions of returnee	Proportion of returnees who (do not) re-migrate	Actual socio-economic status of returnees	Actual persecution or violence against returnees
Aggregate conditions of home country	Trends in levels of emigration and asylum-seeking abroad	Trends in levels of poverty and well-being	Trends in levels of persecution, conflict and violence

Source: Based on Black et al. (2004).

Many definitions, including the IOM approach and other suggestions in the literature, lay out a comprehensive approach to reintegration. The recently released IOM *Handbook on Reintegration* (2019[9]) bases its practical guidance according to these definitions. Nonetheless, there is no standardised understanding of "sustainable return" that serves as a benchmark for most of today's AVRR programmes. This may be related to the fact that many of the definitions provided, while clear, may be challenging to satisfy in many origin-country circumstances and with the means, scope and timeline under which many AVRR programmes operate. Evaluations conducted against these aspirational definitions are likely to find programmes unable to meet the standard of success. The existing definitions of sustainability identify the domains of attention, but the question of how to translate them into practical measurement for AVRR programmes remains and must be answered going forward.

5.1. Definitions of "sustainable" return in national programmes

European countries covered in the OECD study have moved beyond return counselling and assistance, extending support to the re-establishment period in the origin country. This shift is informed by the understanding that return cannot be sustainable if the return migrant is not successfully reintegrated in their origin society. As many irregular migrants and asylum seekers return with significant debts to their communities, sometimes after a long period of absence from the country, and almost always in a difficult psychological state, there are many barriers to return migrants' inclusion in origin country societies, making re-migration more likely. Although all countries make a clear commitment to sustainable reintegration, there is no common definition of "sustainable return or reintegration" across countries visited in this project. The lack of definitions and established indicators for measurement makes comparisons across studies difficult. A common understanding is necessary, but raises the question about who these programmes should be sustainable for: the states administering return and reintegration, the origin countries and communities, or the individual returning migrants themselves.

Some of the elements identified in Table 5.1 can be found in the definitions used by agencies and organisations working on AVRR programming seen in Table 5.2. GIZ, for example, defines sustainable reintegration as the equal participation of returnees and host communities in the social, economic, and political/legal spheres (three dimensions of reintegration) of the origin country. In their understanding, returnees and host communities must have equal access to social services and the labour market. Their definition includes the individual, community levels and at the structural/institutional level. Sustainable reintegration does not preclude the possibility of renewed migration.

Table 5.2. Definitions of sustainable reintegration

Country	Definition
Belgium	The person has a place in its community and has an income. We facilitate sustainability by giving tools to the returnee, but don't measure it.
Denmark	n/a
France	Sustainable reintegration is when the beneficiary of the programme is still in their home country three years after return. For long-term sustainability, the returnee should be helped and supported by those around them. Another factor applying to those with income-generating projects is that the returnee has experience working in the same sector or trade which was identified in the return project.
Germany	GIZ has developed a working definition of sustainable reintegration based on the equal participation of returnees and host communities in the social, economic, and political/legal spheres (three dimensions of reintegration). Only by interlinking these dimensions can the complex development and human rights implications of return flows be addressed. Similarly, the chances of peaceful coexistence are improved with income and employment prospects. To achieve this, returnees and host communities need equal access to social (labour market) services and the corresponding legal framework. Support measures can work at both the individual and community levels and at the structural/institutional level. Sustainable reintegration does not preclude the possibility of renewed migration.
Norway	n/a
Sweden	There is no re-migration and the returning migrant is able to economically support him or herself.
Switzerland	n/a
United Kingdom	Not definition, but "strategic intent": To provide sustainable reintegration support to migrants on return to their country or community of origin. The support aims to help them re-establish their lives and help minimise potential vulnerability, ensuring they have the means to either succeed in their community or country of origin or re-migrate legally and safely, reducing the push factor for irregular re-migration upon return. Done properly, it will reduce pressure on states when receiving their nationals and help developing countries grow economically.

Source: OECD Policy Questionnaire Return and Reintegration 2020.

While some countries and organisations have developed an official understanding of sustainable reintegration, the majority of actors involved in AVRR have not developed a working definition of "sustainable return and reintegration". Fedasil, for example, does not operate under a formal definition of "sustainable reintegration". They do, however, develop their understanding of the concept through various internal trainings and workshops on the topic. Fedasil emphasises the economic, social, and psychosocial dimensions and the importance of including local communities. The French Office for Immigration and Integration does not have a clear definition of "sustainable return" either, but considers return sustainable if an individual remains in their country for a period of three years after return. This has consequences for the actions taken under France's AVRR programme, since under this definition, the creation of income-generating activities requires attention.

From a migration management perspective, sustainability of return may indeed be that people remain in their country of origin and do not re-emigrate. The simplest indicator of success, used for example in France and Sweden, is the lack of re-migration. The French Office for Immigration and Integration does not have an official working definition of "sustainable return" either, but considers return sustainable if an individual remains in their country for a period of three years after return. Under this definition, unsustainable return refers to returnees who do not aim to reintegrate and are able to re-migrate irregularly, either back to the previous destination country or elsewhere. This definition considers "sustainable" the return of those who are unable to re-migrate, regardless of whether they are successfully reintegrated in their origin country – those considered "unsustainably returned" (Strand et al., 2016[2]) when they are not successfully reintegrated, but lack the ability to re-migrate. Most countries acknowledge this risk of unsustainable return in their definition and widen it to include criteria for successful reintegration into the fabric of their origin societies. Both Sweden and France consider economic reintegration, with the idea that people economically able to support themselves and their family are less likely to re-migrate in search of opportunities. This places the emphasis on creation of income-generating activities.

The most comprehensive definitions of "sustainable" reintegration go beyond the generation of income. They include a socio-cultural dimension, require attention to the safety and security, i.e. trust in the government, access to justice, experienced personal harassment since return. Increasingly, different actors call for consideration of a political and legal dimension to "sustainable" reintegration, including access to anti-discrimination remedies and full enjoyment of civil and human rights. Within GIZ's definition, refugees and host communities must have equal access to social services and the labour market. Their definition includes the individual, community levels and the structural/institutional level. Sustainable reintegration under this definition does not preclude the possibility of renewed (legal) migration.

While some countries and organisations have developed an official understanding of sustainable reintegration, the majority of actors involved in AVRR have not developed a working definition of "sustainable return and reintegration". Fedasil, for example, has no mandate for reintegration so does not operate under a formal definition of "sustainable reintegration". They do, however, develop their understanding of the concept through various internal trainings and workshops on the topic. Fedasil emphasises the economic, social, and psychosocial dimensions and the importance of including local communities. Following this understanding, Fedasil facilitates sustainable reintegration by giving tools to the returnee, but there is no attempt to measure the different dimensions. The United Kingdom does not have a definition, but includes a "strategic intent" to foster reintegration by helping returnees to re-establish their lives and help minimise potential vulnerability, reducing the push factor for irregular re-migration upon return. Under this vision, when reintegration is supported properly, it will reduce pressure on states when receiving their nationals and help developing countries grow economically. Similarly, Norway and Switzerland note that sustainable reintegration is the aim of assisted return programmes, but do not have a clear definition of sustainability.

5.2. Reintegration packages: in-kind re-establishment support in country of return

In recent decades, countries have started to go beyond one-time "return packages" limited to cash assistance and costs to realise the return, moving towards offering longer-term assistance to reintegrate return migrants into their origin societies and help them build a sustainable basis for life in their origin country. Enabling migrants to re-establish themselves in the society of their country of origin and empowering them to participate in social, cultural, economic and political life again is a central aim of reintegration assistance. While there is a growing understanding among stakeholders that the reintegration process needs to be supported in order to be successful, the means of doing this differ widely. Without such assistance, sustainable return seems unlikely in most cases – the target populations of return assistance includes populations with difficult characteristics, including individuals who left their respective schooling systems at early stages, and took up substantial debt, including to their family and community, to enable their migration journey. In order to address the difficulties they might face after return, countries offer support through reintegration assistance packages, which include in-kind support for business creation, or medical and housing assistance.

Table 5.3. Levels of in-kind reintegration assistance in origin country

	Reintegration Assistance
Belgium	Base of EUR 700, plus 1 500 for asylum seekers who withdraw their application or depart within 30 days of refusal. Addition support is available for vulnerable cases
Denmark	Up to DKK 20 000, approx. EUR 2 700, per adult and child, through ERRIN and ERSO.
France	Levels of reintegration assistance: • Level 1 (time limit six months): Social assistance- Housing, Medical Assistance, School fees. Up to EUR 400 per adult and EUR 300 per minor (maximum of EUR 3 000 per person for the ERRIN and URA). • Level 2 (time limit one year): Employment assistance- Job search assistance (CV, job interview, contact with companies…). Financing of a training (up to EUR 2 000). Financial assistance to support up to 60% of the salary in the limit of EUR 4 000 (up to EUR 5 000 in special cases; EUR 3 000 maximum/ person in ERRIN and URA). • Level 3 (time limit one year): Starting a business assistance- feasibility study of the project with a local service provider. Support for a training related to the project up to EUR 1 000). Financing the start of the business up to EUR 6 300 (up to EUR 10 000). Support monitoring of the activity for one year (up to 18-24 months).
Germany	In-kind assistance varies on an individual basis according to the programme and eligibility and the country of destination. "StarthilfePlus" programme provides cash assistance (EUR 1 000 for an individual and EUR 2 000 for a family paid 6-8 months after a voluntary departure from Germany) as well as a reintegration component of housing and reintegration assistance for those who were in a long-term tolerated status.
Sweden	Reestablishment support offered in cash, SEK 30 000 per adult and 75 000 per family (EUR 3 000 and 7 500). In-kind support offered through ERRIN (EUR 2 500 for voluntary returns and 2 000 for forced returns).
Switzerland	Individual return assistance up to CHF 3 000 for a social or professional integration project. A project return assistance up to CHF 5 000 for special integration needs.
United Kingdom	For individuals who fall into one of the following three groups, they are eligible for cash/in-kind assistance of the maximum amounts: • Those who are deemed vulnerable (GBP 1 000) • Those who are/ have been in the asylum process (GBP 1 500) • Family members (GBP 2 000) Short term accommodation, education, childcare and business start-up, up to a value of GBP 2 000 is available under VRS.

Source: OECD Policy Questionnaire Return and Reintegration 2020.

Table 5.3 gives an overview of the monetary value of the reintegration assistance provided to returnees beyond administrative and material assistance in preparing the trip to the country of return. Most countries have moved away entirely from cash payments, although there are certain cases, such as in the UK and Sweden, where cash payments are still made under certain circumstances. Regarding assistance 'in kind' compared to 'in cash', the latter provides only for the migrant's immediate needs after arrival, and was more useful than a large cash grant. This means of support avoids putting the migrant under pressure to share money with the extended family and facilitates follow-up and counselling on expenditure.

Some countries refrain from communicating the maximum amount/any fixed amount of assistance to the return migrant during counselling sessions, focusing instead on communicating the opportunities that the assistance can open up in the home country. In many counsellors' experience, communicating the amount of monetary benefits as such leads to misunderstandings when return migrants do not receive the promised assistance in cash, but through material assistance. This approach is notably taken in Germany, where, during counselling, the amount itself is calculated on an individual basis depending on the need and project of the individual, but is never communicated to the individuals themselves. In all other countries, in-kind assistance is based on fixed amounts. The amount is not calibrated according to specific country of origin circumstances and cost of living.

Table 5.4. Eligibility for reintegration support (economic, medical, housing assistance)

Country	Migrants without permission to stay	Migrants with permission to stay	Asylum seekers, pending claim	Asylum seekers, rejected application	Refugees & those with subsidiary protection	Comments
Belgium	Yes	No	Yes	Yes	No	
Denmark						
France	Yes	No	No	Yes	No	
Germany	Yes	Yes	Yes	Yes	Yes	IDPs, returnees from third countries, local population
Norway	Yes	No	Yes	Yes	No	
Sweden	No	No	Yes	Yes	No	
Switzerland						
United Kingdom	Yes	No	Yes	Yes	No	

Source: OECD Policy Questionnaire Return and Reintegration 2020.

In all countries, the same eligibility discussed under the section on return packages applies to reintegration support (see Table 2.1). Similarly, forced returnees are not eligible for reintegration assistance. France offers no reintegration package for forced return, although since July 2019, third country nationals exempt from visa requirements placed in detention centres can apply for an in-cash allowance of EUR 650 at the time of their deportation in France. Germany, on the other hand, does provide reintegration assistance for forced returnees, as their programmes in countries of origin are open to the entire local population. From a development perspective, there are arguments to justify reintegration offers for forced returnees: since forced returns place a harder burden on the returning individual, support in these cases is even more compelling. Ensuring that forced returnees are well reintegrated serves the goal of destination countries seeking to prevent revolving-door migration phenomena.

Further, countries that account for reintegration support as Official Development Assistance (ODA), encounter the problem that excluding deportees from reintegration support introduces a discriminatory element that is not permissible. The eligibility of forced return migrants is thus in line with the methodology and principles of development cooperation, which must be non-discriminatory in the services it offers.

5.3. Obstacles to reintegration: drawing on the literature on employment outcomes for returnees

There is a large literature focusing on the economic impact of return on the development of origin countries, including employment outcomes. The reintegration of returnees into the home labour market is, however, not always as straightforward as some studies suggest, since many do not account for the characteristics of returnees relative to those who migrate. General findings of positive outcomes for return migrants in terms of wages and return on human capital acquired abroad may not apply to the migrants who return under programmes providing reintegration assistance. Findings indicating difficulty with reintegration may be more relevant: for example, those indicating delays to participation in the home labour market if returnees bring skills that do not match the requirements of the home labour market, or if they have higher reservation wages when they return. In some cases, over-qualification can be a problem. Furthermore, entrepreneurship often requires strong social capital, which may have depreciated during migrants' stay abroad (Marchetta, 2012[10]), and may not be the case for migrants for whom the entrepreneurial choice is a reaction to the requirement to return rather than the realisation of the migration project itself. Corruption in the origin country can have psychosocial effects on identity and the sense of belonging, and obstruct entrepreneurship, worsen economic outcomes and job opportunities (Paasche, 2016[11]).

Returnees who particularly face difficulties in re-joining the labour market in their country of origin include those migrants who came to the destination country for non-economic reasons (e.g. asylum seekers) or for those who were forcibly returned. In those cases, where employment opportunities in the home country played no role in return planning, it may be harder to capitalise on the migration experience. Cassarino (2004[12]) discusses this link between reintegration success and the reasons for and types of return. He finds that success of reintegration is determined by the returnee's preparedness, i.e. the willingness and readiness to return. The higher the returnees' preparedness, the more they are able to mobilise resources and are more likely to contribute to economic development in the origin country. Whether a return is forced or voluntary, therefore, has implications on whether the return is sustainable, as noted in a recent study which finds that forced returnees to the Maghreb region are more vulnerable to negative labour market outcomes compared to voluntary returnees (David, 2017[13]).

A specific case of return are situations in which conflict was the original driver of large movements, followed by large-scale return after the end of the conflict. In the context of such large-scale refugee repatriation, the experiences made abroad and the decision to return differ significantly from those of other returning migrants. In a conflict situation, households often leave behind livestock, land, and other assets that are difficult to reclaim in the post-conflict period. Often, the host country also imposes restrictions on the movements and economic activities of refugees (e.g. in camps, but also applies labour market restrictions in non-camp situations), causing long periods of inactivity. These factors might explain the economic gap that Fransen, Ruiz and Vargas-Silva (2017[14]) find in Burundi between returnee households and those who stayed back.

5.4. Economic reintegration: business support and training

All countries participating in the study offered some form of support to promote economic reintegration of returning migrants, by offering opportunities to develop an income generating activity. As discussed above, most programmes now provide in-kind assistance, based on a project developed and approved in the destination country prior to the return. Since the formal sector is often underdeveloped in origin countries, most of these projects aim at business creation, especially in retail and services. The assistance varies according to the project of the return migrant, but generally includes business support, purchase of necessary equipment, fees for required licences, and other essential elements for starting up an activity.

In other cases, training is provided, prior to return where possible and with necessary additional training upon return.

Although all countries included in the study currently have or are considering training programmes for returnees in countries of origin, there are few attempts to join forces across EU or OECD countries, which might enable countries to present more diverse offers or reach more beneficiaries. "Mutualisation" of existing programmes is already in place; France, for example, has multilateral agreements in countries where OFII has no presence. Germany conducts joint work with France in three countries, where they have signed agreements for collaboration. OFII also has agreements to provide services to Austria's reintegration assistance programmes in countries where it is active. At the same time, while the German government is looking for coherence and synergies with other countries, it will continue to pursue bilateral agreements. ERRIN has been an important network in tackling this challenge. The technical working group in ERRIN is currently working on harmonising and mutualising existing programmes, including training and business support; most countries covered in the study support the development of shared initiatives in which they can participate.

In some programmes, returning migrants, together with their return counsellors, work out a business plan that is approved while in the destination country. Generally, this plan needs to be followed upon return, and service providers in the origin country act as business advisors who work with the individual to implement the plan. In other programmes, such as the OFII's, the business plan is developed not in the destination country, but only upon return to the origin country. Projects of OFII beneficiaries, devised together with service providers in the origin country, are approved by a bi-annual selection committee led by respective French ambassadors, including among others, the service provider, OFII representatives and national authorities (e.g. Ministry of Employment or Social affairs representatives).

While there are benefits to designing a plan while in the destination country, especially considering migrants' need for a concrete outlook on post-return life during counselling, the experience of many local implementing partners shows that programmes must include flexibility to adapt to the new realities upon return. Many of the organisations providing business support on the ground reported that a number of returning migrants feel the need to reshape or completely abandon their initial idea upon encountering new circumstances and challenges once in the origin country. The initial idea is important pre-return to build enthusiasm for the return project and to reinforce the sense of agency in the decision, increasing motivation. The need to change the pre-conceived project after return requires mediating potential disappointment and frustration, underlining the need for close support in this phase.

The majority of returnees who receive economic reintegration support turn to entrepreneurship, finding that creating their own business is the best way to overcome labour market re-entry problems. However, in light of high numbers of failed start-ups by return migrants, reintegration programmes are increasingly building in mechanisms to ensure that their business ideas are viable. One major issue in most programmes is that business ideas proposed by returnees are seldom linked to conditions of origin countries, not matching return migrants' actual skills or the needs of the local labour market. In order to overcome this mismatch, programmes have started to analyse skills gaps in local markets, ensuring that migrants and counsellors devise projects in sectors with high demand. For a number of countries, one issue has been trying to go beyond a traditional "catalogue of business ideas". IOM in Switzerland, for example, published a leaflet on success rates of certain business projects in particular countries (certain projects might be viable in one country but not in another, e.g. because of difficulties in acquiring spare parts due to sanction regimes). This approach helps prevent returns from distorting local labour markets through large numbers of returnees concentrating in specific occupations.

One side of avoiding mismatches relates to the needs of the local labour market – the other side concerns the skills the returnee can bring to it. The German-Tunisian Centre for Jobs, Migration and Integration, which provides on-site counselling for returnees seeking job and vocational training opportunities in Tunisia, begins every reintegration counselling process by creating a profile (success prospects, skills, motivation) of the return migrant. This step ensures that counsellors gain a better idea of potential projects that might be suitable for the individual. Counsellors specifically include efforts to identify skills gained abroad, such as language qualifications, which might be sought after by employers in the origin country. Moreover, the initial profiling phase provides assessment of soft skills and suitability for entrepreneurship in terms of personality, conducted by trained psychologists the Centre employs as counsellors. Where necessary, counsellors can connect return migrants to projects that provide opportunities for reskilling: The German Chambers of Commerce Abroad (AHK), for example, operates a reskilling project (CORP Tunisia). Finally, together with feasibility aspects and existing skills, counsellors should not neglect returnees' own wishes and motivation to ensure ownership of project. Generally, the private sector is a potential partner in reintegration, but which has not yet been adequately included in efforts of employment promotion. Another initiative by the AHK in Tunisia is to establish a database of returnees' skills and qualifications and provide access to this information to private sector firms. This database targets local employers in origin countries who may be interested in hiring return migrants who have particular skills related to their stay abroad, such as language skills or familiarity with certain markets and work cultures. Moreover, within the German reintegration programmes, return migrants are linked to employers through job fairs organised by the GIZ in different countries of origin. One recent project for partnering with German businesses and the private sector in the origin country is a pilot run with a large German industrial manufacturing company. As the company is bidding for the reconstruction of electricity networks in Iraq, the GIZ arranged to send 30 returnees to receive training by the company for subsequent employment in Iraq.

Diaspora organisations and ties can also be of assistance in developing and expanding projects. In Kosovo, for example, the large Kosovo diaspora in EU countries is an ideal market for local firms exporting food products but also goods such as restaurant supplies (uniforms, table linen, etc.), drawing on both market knowledge and positive ties.

5.5. Pre-return training: benefits and limits

Reintegration in the country of origin is a process which can start already while in the destination country. Pre-departure assistance provided in donor countries in the context of voluntary returns is indeed considered part of in-donor refugee costs under ODA. For reintegration programmes to be tailored to the individual needs of a returnee, an assessment of the persons' needs, capacities and competencies must be made preferably well in advance of the migrants' return. In order to maximise preparation before departure, the German authorities have gone beyond counselling to offer pre-departure training. Since 2018, they operate a total of 5 000 training opportunities in 15 programmes all across Germany. These programmes are run in training centres that also offer courses aimed at migrants' integration in Germany. Observing that a large share of those in integration classes have no perspective of stay in Germany, the time is being used instead to prepare and train individuals for building a basis for reintegration in their origin country. On the one hand – as supported by evidence in the literature – maximising opportunities for training while increasing preparation for return is believed to raise the prospects for favourable reintegration outcomes. On the other, pre-return training is believed to increase the credibility of the reintegration programme by equipping the returning migrants with a concrete qualification.

Pre-return training faces a number of challenges. First, training costs are generally higher in the host country than in the origin country. A further issue is the high turn-over rates of participants joining and leaving a course frequently. In addition, participation in a course is in most cases not suspensive of removal procedures, so participants remain subject to sudden removal during the course. This argues for short, flexible modules with certificates issued regularly, so that competences can be demonstrated after return.

GIZ, for example, offers skill trainings to support migrants who set up businesses once they return. The duration of the training varies – from two to as many as 12 weeks – although the average is two to three week training. Participants appreciate being able to take the training in Germany, as they typically have time – especially those who do not have legal access to the labour market. Once they return to the country of origin, they may have immediate commitments or complications which prevent participation in training. In addition, the GIZ training is offered to people in accommodation centres even though they do not have access to work, giving them more empowerment in the migration process, and offers a source of stability. Pre-return qualifications are also an effective way to start reflecting on what to do after return.

For asylum applicants who are awaiting a final decision, one question is whether training can be organised for a dual track: applicable for integration if the applicant receives leave to remain, and applicable for reintegration in the origin country in the case of return. For successful integration of those who end up staying, early participation in training is associated with better outcomes. However, the question has come up in some European countries of whether participation in integration courses discourages return in the case of a negative decision. A literature review in response to a Swiss parliamentary query found no evidence that integration courses increase the likelihood of stay in the event of a negative decision (Ruedin et al., 2019[15]).

5.6. Other obstacles to return addressed by reintegration support

Return is often perceived as a failure, by the returning migrant themselves and their communities. Many migrants return in a fragile psychological state, some struggle with mental illnesses. This psycho-social dimension to sustainable reintegration, overcoming trauma, shame and the stigma of return, is increasingly being addressed through awareness raising and psychological counselling and assistance.

The social dimension is key to reintegrating return migrants into their origin communities. The reality is, however, that returnees are not always perceived positively by those who have never migrated. It is a commonly held belief among many that return is in migrants' own hands and signifies failure. Many have the idea that only those people showing problematic behaviour and drawing negative attention, mostly criminals, are made to leave Europe. Within the project, discussions with return migrants in Tunisia reinforced this observation, as many had to struggle with rejection from within their communities, including their own family members. In order to counter this narrative, the Swedish Migration Agency has developed a campaign in Afghanistan that seeks to raise acceptance of returnees in the origin communities, promoting visions of how returnees can be an asset to local communities. By fighting stigmatisation in origin communities, these information campaigns seek to facilitate the social integration of returnees.

Another approach to fighting stigmatisation and rejection is to involve and empower returnees themselves. On the one hand, returnees can be involved in awareness-raising with their communities: this can be an informal role, simply telling their own experiences, although most returnees report that their own stories – however difficult and even harrowing – do little to discourage their peers from the idea of migration. On the other, reintegration or development programmes can support a grassroots model that responds to local communities in the region. The Inter-American Foundation (IAF), for instance, operates no reintegration programmes per se, but provides funding in response proposals by community-led initiatives in Latin America and the Caribbean. Instead of working through large NGOs, it supports organisations that are prioritising grassroots groups. In 2014, a group of returnees funded by the IAD started an initiative to focus on recognising their own experiences in reintegration and make their knowledge available to other returnees, both focusing on the services that should be available, as well as creating direct support channels to recent returnees (See Box 5.1).

Box 5.1. Inter-American Foundation activity to support return migrants in Central America

The Inter-American Foundation (IAF) is a U.S. Government development agency that partners directly with vulnerable populations, grassroots groups and civil society organisations in Latin America and the Caribbean. This complements the traditional model of development cooperation – represented by USAID and other U.S. government agencies. IAF invests in community-led resilience initiatives that reduce the push factors driving irregular migration, including reintegration of returned migrants and opportunities for migrant families in countries of origin. Among the recent grants are two organisations which focus directly on returning migrants and their communities.

The Association of Guatemalan Returnees (ARG), one recipient of support, is an NGO created by Guatemalans returning from the United States. It began to provide spontaneous support to returnees as they arrived at the airport, offering orientation and initial support; it also worked to expand economic reintegration opportunities (to access employment, vocational training, government and community services and emotional support). ARG coordinates with government authorities to gain access to returning migrants at the point of entry and provide support, as well as to provide input to government strategies in this domain. IAF supports ARG to seed microenterprises, support job placement, increase capacity of staff, and work with local governments to support inclusion. It also conducts information campaigns on migration risks in specific locations.

The Alliance of Returned Salvadorans (ALSARE) supports returned migrants with skills and needs assessments, psycho-social assistance, orientation to seed capital and training. It also engages municipal authorities to ensure inclusion in social and economic programmes.

The IAF approach aims to identify grassroots initiatives and support them to expand their activities. In both cases, the civil society organisations aim to participate in policy-making dialogue, increase acceptance of returnees by their communities and in mainstream services and development initiatives. The grants are scaled to the size of the organisations – USD 220 000 in the first case, and 50 000 in the second – but are meant to increase capacity and expand operations, alongside other sources of funding, including co-financing from the associations themselves.

For more information, see www.iaf.gov.

A more direct intervention is offered by URA ("Bridge"), a project created and led by the German Federal Office for Migration and Refugees to promote the reintegration of Kosovan nationals returning from one of the nine partner Federal States. URA's main role is to identify the individual needs of returnees and offer individualised support – e.g psychological support, social counselling, job placement as well as financial support in form of in-kind assistance URA has some discretion to provide support to these individual root causes.

Financial support can lead to tensions between local populations who persevered through poverty, conflict or crisis and populations and returnees receiving financial reintegration assistance. Often, persons in the local community have no understanding for why those who, in their view, had their opportunities to search for better opportunities and "failed", are provided further assistance. This issue is especially salient for public institutions, employment agencies of the origin country in particular, that are involved in administering reintegration support. This problem is encountered by the Tunisian employment agency ANETI, who chose not to propagate assistance publicly.

Certain programmes seek to minimise tensions with local communities by including structural aid for the local community in reintegration packages. Swiss authorities, for example, complement the individual solution – a business project, housing solution and medical support – with structural aid. The return migrant receives their reintegration package; at the same time, their return brings running water and other structural improvements to the village they returned to, supporting the whole community.

Social reintegration and a tight-knit support structure are especially crucial for vulnerable migrants or migrants who have survived violence, for example, trafficking in persons. For these cases, programming must go beyond the usual reintegration package and economic assistance, offering a combination of psychological support and (if applicable) training for employment addressing vulnerabilities. In Germany, some civil society partners specialise in vulnerable groups, including women and victims of trafficking. The trainings offered for vulnerable groups follows an individual approach and are tailored to the capacities and needs of the individual returnee. Victims of trafficking are treated differently in most programmes, and are offered additional support and specialised counselling. In the projects reviewed, their return was seen as more challenging, due to the difficulty of providing support after return. This issue has also been raised in studies (Paasche, Skilbrei and Plambech, 2018[16]).

For some return migrants with medical needs, the traditional reintegration path concentrating on self-sustained employment might not be possible, and require longer-term assistance in local medical systems. Many countries in the project provide adapted or additional support for migrants with specific health needs. Further, reintegration assistance must take into account the needs of returning families. It is crucial to address needs of children returning, e.g. starting at right level of school and at the beginning of school year. Children, sometimes with no recollection of the origin country, are often left out of return process, caught off-guard without adequate preparation. In order to prepare and foster understanding and acceptance of return among returning children, Fedasil has designed a specific booklet together with university researchers. It contains several stages, which return counsellors are to go through meeting by meeting. School placement is one of the main activities of programmes in origin countries, and may require purchasing textbooks and negotiating with local schools to ensure that returning children are enrolled quickly and placed in classes appropriate to their age level.

References

Cassarino, J. (2004), "Theorising Return Migration: The Conceptual Approach to Return Migrants Revisited", *International Journal on Multicultural Societies*, Vol. 6/2, pp. 253-279. [12]

David, A. (2017), "Back to Square One: Socioeconomic Integration of Deported Migrants", *International Migration Review*, Vol. 51/1, pp. 127-154. [13]

European Migration Network (2016), "Guidelines for Monitoring and Evaluation of AVR(R) Programmes", European Commission. [1]

Fransen, S., I. Ruiz and C. Vargas-Silva (2017), "Return Migration and Economic Outcomes in the Conflict Context", *World Development*, Vol. 95, pp. 196-210. [14]

Gesellschaft für Internationale Zusammenarbeit (GIZ) (2018), *Skills for Reintegration Target-Group-Specific Approaches to Reintegration for Education and Technical Vocational Education and Training in Fragile and Conflict-Affected Contexts*. [7]

Graviano, N. and N. Darbellay (2019), "A framework for assisted voluntary return and reintegration", *Migration Policy Practice*, Vol. 9/1, pp. 9-14, https://publications.iom.int/system/files/pdf/mpp_37.pdf. [5]

IOM (2019), *Reintegration Handbook: Practical guidance on the design, implement ation and monitoring of reintegration assistance*, International Organization for Migration, Geneva. [9]

IOM (2017), *Towards an Integrated Approach to Reintegration in the context of return*, International Organisation for Migration (IOM), http://www.iom.int/sites/default/files/our_work/DMM/AVRR/Towards-an-Integrated-Approach-to-Reintegration.pdf. [4]

Koser, K. and K. Kuschminder (2015), *Comparative Research on the Assisted Voluntary Return and Reintegration of Migrants*, International Organization for Migration, Geneva. [6]

Kuschminder, K. (2017), "Interrogating the Relationship between Remigration and Sustainable Return", *International Migration*, Vol. 55/6. [3]

Lenoël, A., M. Şerban and A. Vandenbunder (2018), "Report on Non-Economic Impacts of Temporary, Circular and Permanent Migration", *Working Paper Series Temporary versus Permanent Migration*, No. 12, EU Temper Project. [8]

Marchetta, F. (2012), "Return Migration and the Survival of Entrepreneurial Activities in Egypt", *Etudes et Documents,*, No. 17, CERDI. [10]

Paasche, E. (2016), "The role of corruption in reintegration: experiences of Iraqi Kurds upon return from Europe", *Journal of Ethnic and Migration Studies*, Vol. 42/7, pp. 1076-1093, http://dx.doi.org/10.1080/1369183X.2016.1139445. [11]

Paasche, E., M. Skilbrei and S. Plambech (2018), "Vulnerable Here or There? Examining the vulnerability of victims of human trafficking before and after return", *Anti-Trafficking Review* 10, http://dx.doi.org/10.14197/atr.201218103. [16]

Ruedin, D. et al. (2019), *Corrélations entre migration, intégration et retour*, Institut SFM, Neuchâtel. [15]

Samuel Hall and IOM (2017), *Setting standards for an integrated approach to reintegration.* [17]

Strand, A. et al. (2016), "Programmes for assisted return to Afghanistan, Iraqi Kurdistan, Ethiopia and Kosovo: A comparative evaluation of effectiveness and outcomes", *CMI Report R 2016:2*, Chr, Michelsen Institute. [2]

Notes

1 Global Compact for Safe, Orderly and Regular Migration, Objective 21, Final draft, 11 July 2018. https://refugeesmigrants.un.org/sites/default/files/180711_final_draft_0.pdf. The Global Compact was endorsed by 164 countries in December 2018.

6 Partnerships with origin country authorities

Origin countries are responsible for providing equal access to services to their own nationals returning from abroad. In the framework of reintegration assistance programmes, destination countries can cooperate on migration objectives. Development cooperation can contribute to the capacity of origin country institutions to address the needs of returning migrants, at the policy and the implementation level. Reintegration assistance programmes can partner and coordinate with origin country services and transfer case management.

Sustainable return and reintegration depends not only on cooperation within destination country administrations, but partnership with origin countries – for return, but particularly when it comes to longer-term reintegration from a development perspective. Successful return requires origin countries' cooperation in readmission, but sustainable reintegration programmes need to foster ownership by local and national authorities and other stakeholders in countries of origin, in particular through institutional capacity-building activities. In the long term, returnees cannot be indefinitely supported – financially or otherwise – through programmes and initiatives run by destination countries. With this goal in mind, existing reintegration programmes must create connections to local structures and processes in origin countries, ultimately aiming at a handover to local authorities and actors. The country of origin is responsible for its own citizens after return, no more and no less than it is responsible for its own citizens who have not migrated.

6.1. Cooperation on migration objectives

While return and the reintegration of returnees is a high priority policy issue in the destination country, and brought to the origin country as a priority issue, it often appears lower on the agenda of many origin countries, both in terms of public perception and policy maker priorities. In addition, countries of origin and countries of destination might further vary substantially in their understanding of return migration and reintegration of returning migrants. Many European countries have undertaken efforts to set the framework for activity in origin countries in migration dialogues or readmission agreements with country of origin authorities, which includes joint efforts at the EU level.

Countries of origin and countries of destination vary substantially in their understanding of return migration and reintegration of returning migrants. For many countries of origin, return is a low priority policy issue, eclipsed by the particularly contentious question of forced return (Haase and Honerath, 2016[1]). Many AVRR programmes aim at facilitating cooperative and coherent policy approaches between the countries involved. At the same time, facilitation of return to countries of origin has been used as a political instrument and bargaining chip in discussions and agreements between states on different forms of cooperation, including explicit or implicit conditionality (D'Humières, 2018[2]; Latek, 2017[3]). Some European governments are taking an explicit "more-for-more" approach in linking concerns of return to development aid, although there is a rejection of the use of aid as a "sanction".

In order to foster ownership and design programmes that are sensitive to contexts in different countries migrants return to, the dialogue on reintegration has attempted to take into account the perspectives and interests of the countries of origin (Federal Ministry of Economic Cooperation and Development (BMZ), 2018[4]; 2019[5]). In order to design partnerships that ensure the sustainability of programming in the long-term, host countries have experimented with models for receiving input from key stakeholders in origin countries. Such input can be found in the outcomes of past dialogues in the form of technical workshops, for example between the African Union and the European Union, identifying challenges, good practices and recommendations for including return migrants into existing labour markets and strengthening institutional capacities (African Union, 2018[6]; 2018[7]; AU, EU, 2018[8]).

Some European governments seek to facilitate agreements on co-operation based on explicit or implicit conditionality. Most notably, Denmark has developed a "flexible return fund" to incentivise origin countries' cooperation on return issues. The fund has been growing since its inception in 2017. It is administered in a "more-for-more" approach in linking concerns of return to development aid, rejecting of the use of aid as a "sanction". Through these migration dialogues, the Danish government does not seek formal readmission agreements, but to arrive at an informal understanding on what the practical issues in cooperation on return and readmission are in a particular origin country, ascertaining how Denmark can support to help facilitate readmission.

At the same time, discussions in several countries have explored whether "less-for-less" approaches would be possible in principle. Besides ethical considerations, it seemed clear that the majority of the existing development portfolio, humanitarian aid in particular, would need to be continued, as they address migration drivers that also hinder motivation to return. A "less-for-less" approach would require wider agreement with development colleagues outside the return and reintegration area, dealing with more structural issues of development cooperation. These actors are unlikely to see the benefit in cutting aid in order to enable the return of a limited number of irregular migrants, especially when that might have wider political repercussions. Lastly, a difficulty of applying a "less-for-less" approach in readmission negotiations is that there is often no overlap between countries where development cooperation is already active and countries where irregular migrants need to return.

While Denmark has most extensively institutionalised linkage of development aid and readmission negotiations among countries participating in this report, others have also seen political forces press to make development assistance conditional on readmission. However, even if this were possible, aid-conditionality is difficult to implement, particularly in light of multi-year planning in development – agencies have large parts of their budget reserved and are rarely flexible. Furthermore, while even smaller OECD countries may be present in a range of origin countries, they rarely count among the top three donors in any of them, limiting their influence and leverage in migration dialogues.

As facilitation of returns has become a more important policy priority for donor countries in their relations with origin countries, contrasting objectives have emerged. Origin countries may not assign the same importance to the reintegration of returning migrants. Returns from European countries, whether forced or not, may be a lower priority; returns from non-OECD destinations are a much larger phenomenon for countries like Afghanistan, Nigeria and Senegal, for example (Samuel Hall, 2020[9]; 2020[10]; Castagnone and Ferro, 2020[11]). Internally displaced persons may be seen as a priority for national programmes (Arrat, 2020[12]). In some cases, such as Kosovo, return migrants from Europe are the main channel and return in such large numbers that they indeed represent a policy priority in the origin country. Bilateral and multilateral dialogue and agreement between European countries and African countries has seen the issue of return and readmission figure among European priorities. Return and readmission are included in the 2000 Cotonou agreement between the EU and the African, Caribbean and Pacific Group of States, although the treaty goes far beyond cooperation on migration. More recently, reintegration has been included in migration-related EU dialogues with African countries: foremost in the 2015 Valletta Summit, where the Emergency Trust fund to promote development in Africa included an aim to cooperate more closely on return, readmission and reintegration.

A further issue is the multitude of different donor countries and the multiplication of partners active in the country of origin. Each donor country has its own programme priorities; many donor countries have different contact points for development, migration and security cooperation, sometimes without strong coordination among them. Even when there is a single voice on the side of a donor country, or a single contact point for initiatives shared among donor countries, there may be multiple contact points for the origin country, representing different institutions.

The presence of reference to reintegration policy in national strategy documents of origin countries is not necessarily a sign of political ownership or that the country assigns a priority to reintegration. Many of the national strategies in origin countries have been developed with financial support from donor countries and with technical support from international organisations, which guarantees inclusion of reference to reintegration as part of international good practice and as a means to ensure that external support for such measures – in bilateral agreements and in cooperation – aligns with official policy in the origin country. High-level coordination and policy commitment may also be visible to international actors in the country, but remain poorly connected with CSOs and other organisations active at the community level. In Afghanistan, for example, NGOs are largely unrepresented in the Displacement and Returnees Executive Committee (DiREC), the platform for coordinating government and international partner collaboration (Samuel Hall, 2020[10]).

The different forms of collaboration between destination and origin governments, at different levels, of IOM and other international organisations, of CSOs and the private sector, have not been fully investigated or evaluated. While it is apparent that no single model will be applicable in all contexts, some approaches have achieved more success than others. One example of how such multi-level cooperation could work in practice is the "National Reintegration Mechanism" in Tunisia, which involves several destination country agencies, the European Union, multiple local authorities, and implementing partners from civil society (Hammouda, 2020[13]; Muyle, 2018[14]). Not all origin country partners are involved in the mechanism; some continue to work outside of it.

6.2. Building capacity of origin country institutions

The shift in reintegration assistance from cash to in-kind services necessitated a change in the way that programmes interact with countries of origin. Cash payments require limited infrastructure in the country of origin, beyond the administrative capacity for disbursal over time and to conduct any checks foreseen by evaluation. In-kind programmes require partnerships with actors in the origin country, including the coordinating service provider, which range from international organisations and representatives of the host countries and origin countries to CSOs. In addition, they require partnerships with the actors providing reintegration support directly to the returnee, which may include government partners or non-government actors in civil society and the private sector (Figure 6.1). Resources allocated to services can help build capacity beyond service provision to the individual beneficiaries of the programme, even when these investments are not sufficient to build a long-term reintegration infrastructure on their own.

Figure 6.1. Reintegration assistance requires many partners and coordination

Partners involved in providing reintegration assistance and supporting reintegration in the origin country

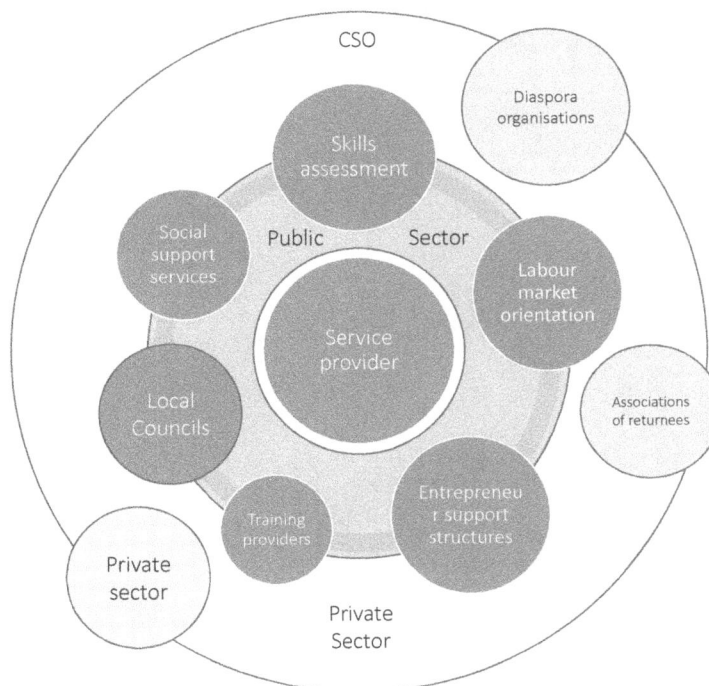

Source: OECD Secretariat

Return and reintegration programmes as described are often narrow in scope, rarely provide structural support to the countries of origin, and often lack individual support over longer periods. In order for individual support and counselling to lead to sustainable reintegration, the beneficiary should be linked to local structures and services. The comprehensive approach for local development and structural long term support in countries of origin lies behind the BMZ programme "Returning to New Opportunities", which aims to support training and employment as well as social support and opening these up to returnees. The programme is linked to existing projects focusing on the institutional, legislative and structural improvement of labour markets, vocational education or municipal development, and its main structures – Advice centres – are designed to work alongside and in coordination with local institutions (Box 6.1).

With this goal in mind, existing reintegration programmes must create connections to local structures and processes in origin countries, ultimately aiming at a handover to local authorities and actors. In the German model, reintegration support is implemented in close cooperation with origin country institutions, such as the ANETI employment agency in Tunisia (Hammouda, 2020[13]). Within this approach, German authorities stress "state-to-state" cooperation, supporting origin-country led national plans such as the Tunisian ANETI's 2030 strategy. A similar approach can be seen in Senegal, where the national body responsible for providing returnees with economic, social and psychosocial support, the Office of Reception and Orientation (BAOS), suffers from low visibility and limited operational capacity (Samuel Hall, 2020[9]). Anchoring the reintegration support offer in existing public institutions and their programmes and building those institutions capabilities lays the groundwork for an "exit" and handover to origin country institutions.

Norway, for example, conducts smaller-scale and more select capacity-building exercises in areas that origin countries have flagged during "migration dialogues". Together with IOM, Norway implemented training for Somali immigration authorities who receive back returnees. A common request for capacity building to handle return amongst country of origin authorities are different forms of police cooperation. Overall, the Norwegian experience seems to have shown that such interventions improve the atmosphere of cooperation and facilitate the functioning of the return process. Such interventions are particularly useful for countries which have small return caseloads and which can benefit from close relationships with gatekeeping authorities in the origin countries.

> **Box 6.1. Advice Centres for Jobs, Migration, and Reintegration in Origin countries**
>
> The centrepiece of the German Federal Ministry for Economic Cooperation and Development programme Returning to New Opportunities are the advice centres opened in countries of origin. The centres are open to the general public in the country, work alongside and in coordination with origin country institutions, and draw on a network of contacts for referral.
>
> The programme Returning to New Opportunities is not directly designed to increase the number of returns, but to improve the entire infrastructure for supporting jobs in the origin country, with a particular but not exclusive attention to the specific needs of returning migrants – whether from Germany or from other countries, including transit countries. The centres also offer expertise in addressing the specific characteristics (experiences, competences and needs) of returnees from Germany.
>
> The first centre, created in Kosovo, provides an example. DIMAK (German Information Centre for Migration, Training and Career). DIMAK provides individual advice about opportunities in Kosovo for employment and training. It orients and refers to training provided by different actors, including those offered by GIZ but also other partners. DIMAK also provides psychosocial support to enter the labour market. It works with the Kosovar Ministry of Labour and Social Welfare.
>
> In Tunis, the German-Tunisian Centre for Jobs, Migration and Reintegration (CTA) is open to the public in the same building as an office of the public employment service ANETI. As in Kosovo, it provides general services and targeted support to returnees from Germany and other countries, as well as the local population.
>
> In Senegal, the Senegalese-German Centre for Jobs, Migration and Reintegration (CSAEM) operates in a similar way. The formal labour market is undeveloped and orientation is, as in other countries, towards self-employment and small-business creation. Return migrants are largely from areas outside the capital, so the centre also works to address the needs of returnees in rural areas through partnerships with regional actors.
>
> Returnees from Germany should have been referred or linked to centres prior to return for example through intermediaries such as the reintegration scouts or return counsellors, since the centre is the contact point for reintegration assistance following return. It can provide information to potential returnees still in Germany, and has access to information provided prior to return. Psychosocial support has turned out to be very important to achieve an acceptance of return. Targeted support measures have been developed for women, as well as for those with special psychological or health needs.
>
> Centres serve other users; indeed, most clients are not return migrants, but local residents who have never left. The majority of users contacting and visiting the Centre come to seek advice for legal migration to Germany; most do not meet criteria for any German legal migration programme. The Centre works to orient them towards other opportunities, especially training. Centres have ties with local actors, especially the local German chambers of commerce, which are often able to provide opportunities, particularly to persons with German experience and training.
>
> The centres are active on social media and respond to contacts.

Another means for capacity building is to administer reintegration assistance jointly with institutions in the origin country. Two examples of this can be found in Tunisia and Kosovo, where commissions involving donor representatives and staff of relevant institutions decide on the range of interventions to provide to individuals receiving assistance. In Tunisia, the commissions operate in the framework of the National Reintegration Mechanism, and are hosted by ANETI but involve case workers from the reintegration programme as well as other relevant services (Hammouda, 2020[13]). The commission reviews the needs of the returnee and validates the reintegration plan, before transferring it as appropriate to an implementing partner responsible for coordinating the case. In Kosovo, a similar approach is taken at the municipal level, where caseworkers evaluate needs and establish a plan, drawing on resources provided by the reintegration programme but also using public services to which returnees have rights. The commission model is one way to deal with the problem of coordination among actors, since there remain many different services and partners, but a single institutional interlocutor for case management.

References

African Union (2018), *The AU Member States Workshop On Reintegration of Returning Migrants into the Labour Market: Outcome Document*. [6]

African Union Commission (2018), *Key Measures for Sustainable Reintegration of Returning Migrants into the Labour Market. Outcomes of the technical workshop on "Reintegration of Returning Migrants in the Labour Market - Scoping the Field"*. [7]

Arrat, E. (2020), *Effective Policies and Programs in the Successful and Sustainable Reintegration of Iraqi Returnees from OECD Countries: Report for the OECD*. [12]

AU, EU, I. (2018), *AU-EU technical workshoAU-EU technical workshop on sustainable reintegration. Within the Framework of the AU-EU-UN Taskforce to Address the Situation of Migrants in Libya*. [8]

Castagnone, E. and A. Ferro (2020), *Return and Sustainable Reintegration: Report on the Nigeria-Germany corridor*, OECD, Paris. [11]

D'Humières, V. (2018), "European Union/African Cooperation: the externalisation of Europe's migration policies", *European Issues*, No. 472, Fondation Robert Schuman, Brussels. [2]

Federal Ministry of Economic Cooperation and Development (BMZ) (2019), *Return and Reintegration of Migrants: A European Dialogue*. [5]

Federal Ministry of Economic Cooperation and Development (BMZ) (2018), *Return and Reintegration of Migrants: A European Dialogue*. [4]

Haase, M. and P. Honerath (2016), *Return Migration and Reintegration Policies. A primer*, Deutsche Gesellschaft für Internationale Zusammenarbeit. [1]

Hammouda, H. (2020), *Retour et Réintegration Durable en Tunisie*, OECD, Paris. [13]

Latek, M. (2017), *Briefing Reintegration of Returning Migrants*, European Parliamentary Research Service. [3]

Muyle, M. (2018), *Cartographie des Acteurs et des Dispositifs Européens de la Réinsertion des Migrants Tunisiens de Retour*, Office Francais de l'Immigration et de l'Integration. [14]

Samuel Hall (2020), *Corridor Report on Sustainable Return and Reintegration: Afghanistan*, OECD, Paris. [10]

Samuel Hall (2020), *Corridor Report on Sustainable Return and Reintegration: Senegal*, OECD, Paris. [9]

7 Evaluation of return and reintegration policies

There are different ways in which reintegration assistance is evaluated. The primary indicator is the outcome of the beneficiary. A framework developed by IOM covering different dimensions provides a detailed overview of some aspects. The many different objectives of reintegration assistance programmes require additional forms of evaluation, including cost-benefit analysis and measuring the impact on communities.

OECD Member States implementing AVRR programmes must demonstrate their effectiveness in achieving the intended objectives and the efficiency with which they can do so. Clearly articulating the desired results is the first step to achieving sustainable reintegration. The next steps are long-term, systematic and comprehensive data-collection and monitoring and evaluation schemes to help assess the relevance, effectiveness, and impact of voluntary return and reintegration assistance.

From the perspective of policy makers, evaluations must assess the extent to which planned results were achieved, as well as the extent to which the resources/inputs (funds, expertise, time) were justified, given the effects that have been achieved. More global evaluations of the sustainability of AVRR programmes are yet to be developed, but are crucial amidst concerns raised as to programmes' effectiveness, cost-efficiency and potential to produce side-effects (e.g. repeat migration or return shopping).

Individual projects and programmes providing AVRR have their own evaluation goals, generally in line with the working definitions of sustainability – explicit or implied – within the project. More broadly, there are examples of evaluation grids designed to be used across projects and platforms established to monitor AVRR.

The two main frameworks for evaluating AVRR activities are beneficiary based (looking at inputs and outcomes at the individual level) and community based (examining the impact on institutions and systems outside of the individual participants). Reflecting the objective of most host-country initiatives, the principal evaluation approach is beneficiary based.

7.1. Beneficiary-based evaluation

In programmes where individuals receive benefits, monitoring and evaluation of individual experience and outcomes is usually built into the programme. Many evaluations also follow up with beneficiaries with questionnaires. In addition, outside evaluations target beneficiaries with batteries of varying dimensions.

One example of beneficiary follow-up is the German Federal Ministry Office for Migration and Refugees Research Central collaboration with IOM to evaluate the programme StarthilfePlus (Schmitt, Bitterwolf and Baraulina, 2019[1]). The evaluation is designed as a longitudinal study, covering as many as 1 740 returnees, and is part of a broader long-term research initiative on return. The survey aims to shed light on reintegration processes and capture further mobility of returnees.

Within its Mediterranean Sustainable Integration (MEASURE) project, funded by DFID, IOM launched a study conducted by Samuel Hall which proposed a new scale of indicators to capture reintegration sustainability both on different levels (individual and community) and along dimensions (economic, social and psychosocial). It includes both qualitative and quantitative indicators, which feed into a reintegration scoring that seeks to allow for an aggregated and standardised understanding of returnees' reintegration outcomes (Samuel Hall and IOM, 2017[2]). The IOM reintegration sustainability survey includes 15 indicators, which were developed and tested in the field, measured by 30 elements of reintegration at an individual level. The measurement elements are based on the returnees' own perceptions of their environment or self-evaluation of their situation. The resulting AVRR "Reintegration Score" comprises three-dimensional scores (measuring reintegration in the economic, social and psychosocial dimensions) and one composite reintegration score that provides a numerical measure of overall reintegration across dimensions (Box 7.1).

Box 7.1. Building a quantitative measure of reintegration

The IOM-Samuel Hall "Sustainable Reintegration Score" and the Reintegration Sustainability Survey

IOM, in collaboration with Samuel Hall, developed a Reintegration Sustainability Survey and related scoring system, which seeks to provide an aggregated and standardised understanding of an AVRR beneficiary's level of reintegration and to answer the question of the extent to which they have achieved a level of sustainable reintegration in communities to which they return.

The scoring system covers 15 indicators covering the economic, social and psychosocial dimensions. It is built based on individual-level indicators based on the returnees' own perceptions of their environment or self-evaluation of their own situation, as well as community-level indicators. By example, the five indicators for the economic dimension are shown in Table 7.1.

Table 7.1. Example of measurement elements for the economic dimension

Indicators	Measurement Elements
Economic Dimension	Measurement (0 to 1, 0=worst situation and 1=best)
1. Source of Income	Currently working (0.1)
	Owns a productive asset (0.1)
2. Reliability and adequacy of employment or income-generating activity	Currently seeking a job (0.1)
	5-point scale based on perception of access to employment/training
3. Debt-to-spending ratio	Household debt does not exceed monthly spending (0.1)
	5-point scale based on frequency of money borrowed (1=never)
	Access to credit if needed (0.1)
4. Food security	5-point scale on frequency of use of food coping mechanisms by family
5. Self-assessment of satisfaction with economic situation	5-point scale based on perception question of economic situation

Source: (Samuel Hall and IOM, 2017[2]).

In addition to providing a score of each of the three dimensions, a "Reintegration Sustainability Score" is calculated, ranging from 0 to 1, based on all 15 indicators. The score is calculated from each dimension, applying weights. It is possible to calculate a composite reintegration score, or scores for each of the three dimensions in order to identify areas where a returnee is particularly vulnerable (Majidi and Nozarian, 2019[3]).

The "Reintegration Sustainability Score" is divided into a global score, which potentially allows for a comparison of trends in beneficiaries' reintegration across country contexts and over time and can be used by case managers.

The Reintegration Sustainability Survey and related scoring system has been institutionalised was operationalised in the field globally by IOM since early 2018. One example is the ORION (Operationalizing an Integrated Approach to Reintegration project) project, in three African countries used the survey, first as a baseline to select those with the lowest reintegration scores for a mentoring approach; then for case management of these beneficiaries (at three-month intervals); and finally for comparative analysis, to compare scores of beneficiaries who received reintegration assistance through different approaches and in different contexts. The scores are also implemented across EU-IOM Actions. The system is incorporated in IOM's institutional information management system. It has also been published through the 2019 Reintegration Handbook as a tool for monitoring reintegration assistance.

Collecting the information requires an interview with the participant which lasts approximately 40 minutes. Some of the questions are personal and require the respondent, for example, to rate their social network in terms of the support it is providing, or to categorise the frequency of situations of conflict. The respondent is given the option of not answering.

Source: (Samuel Hall and IOM, 2017[2]; IOM, 2019[4]).

In 2016, the European Migration Network (EMN) released guidelines for the monitoring and evaluation of AVR(R) programmes that provide a list of questions and indicators to be included in post-return monitoring activities (European Migration Network, 2016[5]). The overall aim of these guidelines is to identify a common methodology for monitoring and evaluation that Member States can apply on a voluntary basis. Specifically, the guidelines propose a common set of core indicators for monitoring and evaluation, which – if applied consistently in all EU Member States – are meant to enable the analysis of EU-level aggregate data on AVR(R) programmes. Further, use of a common methodology is believed to better enable Member States to design and implement joint reintegration projects.

The EMN guidelines cover beneficiary-based evaluation. They respond to the objectives of increasing uptake of AVR(R), successful case management within programmes, and measuring individual outcomes for beneficiaries. The long list of different evaluation questions is matched to corresponding indicators, although collecting the information requires not only a long beneficiary survey following return but also in-depth information from programme operators. Overall, most beneficiaries of return and reintegration assistance – as most returns from Europe – are men. The need to better cover women has been raised (Samuel Hall, 2018[6]; Strand et al., 2016[7]) especially as results suggest that their requirements, outcome and experience are distinct from that of male returnees.

Among the important evaluation questions included in the EMN guidelines is "Are AVR(R) programmes targeting the most relevant beneficiaries (or are they targeting those who would have returned anyway without assistance)". In this case, response is drawn from self-reported motivations for return. To better understand those "who would have returned anyway", it is necessary to also look at other returns (spontaneous, unassisted but also forced) and non-returnees who are part of the target population. Comparative evaluation on these different groups is complex and expensive. One ongoing attempt to compare with a control group is by Sweden's DELMI which has begun surveying assisted and non-voluntary unassisted returnees in the origin country; the output however is expected to inform the assistance programme rather than identify the role that assistance played.

When potential returnees are randomly assigned to different partners for counselling and support, variations in return rates – "conversions" – might reflect the role of information. Just as individual counsellors have varying success, so do different organisations. Many programmes, however, triage potential returnees for referral to specialised partners. Without an understanding of the relative difficulty of conversion for different categories, it is difficult to set a benchmark. A low rate may reflect factors outside of the programme and services, depending on the gap between conditions in the origin and host country and on the risk of removal.

Fedasil in Belgium developed the digital Transition to Reintegration Assistance Tool (RIAT) to support its own work (see Box 3.3). RIAT has been further developed in cooperation with the European Commission and the European Return and Reintegration Network (ERRIN). RIAT is an online tool to manage and follow-up cases of persons that return with reintegration support, which can be adapted to different national settings. It is supposed to facilitate the exchange of information on individual reintegration projects throughout application (before departure), reintegration plan (after arrival) and final reporting.

When timely and low-cost departure is the main objective of offering programmes, it is important to understand the reference cost and to calculate total programme costs. For example, Canada's Border

Services Agency ran a pilot reintegration assistance programme starting in 2012, aimed at failed asylum seekers and using IOM as the service provider. The objective was to accelerate departures and reduce costs. An evaluation after the first two years found that the programme did not reduce the time for departure (appeals continued as previously) and examined the relative cost per removal with benchmark low-risk and high risk removals; the staff cost in terms of paperwork per case was higher than for low risk removals but 29% the cost of high risk removals – in line with "Other countries with voluntary removal programs [where] per-return costs [which] cost about one third the cost of a high-risk removal." (Canada Border Services Agency (CBSA), 2014[8]). However, since the programme involved many applicants who dropped out after paperwork was filed, the programme had additional staff costs. This example is relevant, since many assisted reintegration programmes see dropout throughout the procedure, sometimes right up to the moment of departure.

The above are examples of indicators used and the approaches to measure them. The feasibility of collecting information through these different indicators is not always addressed. Open questions include how to track returnees, who may be highly mobile and hard to reach, and how to structure incentives for them to provide information, especially when they are not receiving support. This is a challenge not limited to the European AVRR context. A United States GAO report on an IOM-implemented programme to support reintegration in the Northern Triangle noted that "determining the effectiveness of reintegration efforts is challenging because of the difficulties of tracking migrants once they return to their communities and of accounting for the various external factors that influence an individual's decision to migrate again" (United States Government Accountability Office, 2018[9]).

Sharing data among partners is complex due to data protection and consent requirements, but it is further complicated when origin country institutions are participants in reintegration assistance programmes, providing services and collecting data. Authorities in origin countries partnering in implementation of programmes collect case information on their own nationals but may be unable or unwilling to report this information. In some origin countries, data protection is a question of sovereignty: there can be no obligation to report on nationals to foreign states, including donors. As involvement of origin country institutions is a long-term objective for some reintegration programmes, the limit on data sharing is a potential barrier to case management and to programme monitoring and evaluation, especially when donors are involved. Even in the case of an official agreement to share certain information, public officials co-ordinating cases and programmes may resent an obligation to report on their nationals to foreign authorities. Other questions revolve around ethical issues when collecting data at the individual level, as the collection and storage of data on a marginalised population is a sensitive matter.

Furthermore, most monitoring tools in use have a limited time horizon (usually 12 months), corresponding to the duration of reintegration support. This horizon may be too short or arbitrary, but there is little evidence on the appropriate time horizon for reintegration monitoring. Indeed, each individual case is different. While there is evidence that the reintegration process is not linear (i.e. returnees do not start from zero and steadily become more reintegrated), but rather contains key "up" and "down" moments over time, this aspect must be better incorporated into evaluation and measurement (Samuel Hall and IOM, 2017[2]).

Reintegration support involves provision of services and financial resources and requires reporting on expenditures and activities, including reporting on the beneficiary. The individual outcome of the beneficiary of reintegration support is the simplest and most obvious measure by which programmes are monitored. As a result, of the focus of monitoring and evaluation has been on beneficiary monitoring, i.e. the sustainability of reintegration for the individual returning migrant.

The EMN guidelines do not address programme implementation arrangements in the origin country, such as services provided by the origin country or by the implementing partner, nor do they address questions related to the community around the beneficiary.

IOM's 2019 results-monitoring framework gives as an example the outcome of community-based reintegration measures and possible associated indicators (IOM, 2019[4]). It also mentions the outcome of measures aimed at capacity-building and awareness raising among different stakeholders.

7.2. Evaluation beyond the impact on beneficiaries

Compared with individual outcomes, less attention has been given to the evaluation of sustainability of reintegration programmes from a technical, but also a financial and political point of view. Positive individual reintegration outcomes for beneficiaries are worthwhile goals, but for most of the host country institutions funding the programme, a positive individual reintegration is not the objective. Rather, the positive individual outcome is interesting to the extent that it supports the entire migration and asylum framework, bolstering integrity of the system and facilitating actors involved in compliance. The success of individual returnees is celebrated, but only to the extent that it contributes to other objectives. Among the different objectives of financing reintegration assistance are: increasing or accelerating return, at a lower financial, political and social cost than alternatives such as forced return or regularisation; reducing remigration; improving relations with origin countries; allowing countries to demonstrate a humanitarian concern in migration enforcement; meeting international commitments such as those contained in the Global Compact on Migration; and reinforcement of policy coherence between migration and development objectives. These objectives are not mutually exclusive.

Assessment of the effectiveness of programmes in accelerating and increasing returns, at lower costs, requires additional data relative to most current platforms. It is important to quantify the delay to departure, and whether this occurs before or after a final asylum decision. On the cost side, for persons in reception centres or receiving other services, the duration of stay is an important indicator of the cost of non-return; even accelerating return decisions by a few months can represent a significant costs savings. Accounting for changes in the time to departure can be as significant as an increase in total returns.

Similarly, triage of returnees according to the relative complexity of their cases and the difficulty of alternative solutions is important. Family units from countries which do not easily cooperate in readmission, for example, represent a greater success in terms of return than the same number of single people from countries with which readmission is straightforward.

In this light, the main interest in the sustainable reintegration of beneficiaries may lie for some programmes in the case it makes for other beneficiaries to take up the return offer. Being able to tell success stories is a key campaign point for some programmes. In other cases, information circulating within migrant and diaspora communities brings reports of success to the host country and raises interest.

The political cost of returns is also to be considered: forced returns of some categories of potential beneficiary may be negatively perceived. Evaluations should try to take into account the impact of reintegration programmes on public perception of the migration system as fair and humane. As these programmes are little known, and perceived primarily in their utility as a means to favour return.

Improved relations with origin countries can take many forms, some of which may go beyond the return domain into broader cooperation on migration management and even security. It is simpler to assess the level of cooperation in public domains than those in which cooperation is invisible, but at least the facility of collaboration on returns should be considered.

References

Canada Border Services Agency (CBSA) (2014), *Evaluation of the Assisted Voluntary Return and Reintegration Pilot Program - Final Report*, Canada Border Services Agency (CBSA), Ottawa, https://www.cbsa-asfc.gc.ca/agency-agence/reports-rapports/ae-ve/2014/avrrpp-pparvr-eng.html (accessed on 9 August 2020). [8]

European Migration Network (2016), *Guidelines for Monitoring and Evaluation of AVR(R) Programmes*, https://ec.europa.eu/home-affairs/sites/homeaffairs/files/what-we-do/networks/european_migration_network/reports/docs/emn-studies/guidelines_for_monitoring_and_evaluation_final_jan2016.pdf (accessed on 23 December 2019). [5]

IOM (2019), *Reintegration Handbook: Practical guidance on the design, implement ation and monitoring of reintegration assistance*, International Organization for Migration, Geneva. [4]

Majidi, N. and N. Nozarian (2019), "Measuring sustainable", *Migration Policy Practice*, Vol. 9/1, pp. 30-39, https://publications.iom.int/system/files/pdf/mpp_37.pdf. [3]

Samuel Hall (2018), *Supporting post-return interventions in Afghanistan-GIZ's Programme for Migration and Development (PME)*. [6]

Samuel Hall and IOM (2017), *Setting standards for an integrated approach to reintegration*. [2]

Schmitt, M., M. Bitterwolf and T. Baraulina (2019), *Geforderte Rückkehr aus Deutschland: Motive und Reintegration. Eine Begleitstudie zum Bundesprogramm StarthilfePlus (Forced return from Germany: Motives and reintegration. Study accompanying the federal program StarthilfePlus)*, Bundesamt für Migration und Flüchtlinge (BAMF), https://www.bamf.de/SharedDocs/Anlagen/DE/Forschung/Forschungsberichte/fb34-evaluation-starthilfeplus.pdf (accessed on 7 August 2020). [1]

Strand, A. et al. (2016), "Programmes for assisted return to Afghanistan, Iraqi Kurdistan, Ethiopia and Kosovo: A comparative evaluation of effectiveness and outcomes", *CMI Report R 2016:2*, Chr, Michelsen Institute. [7]

United States Government Accountability Office (2018), *USAID Assists Migrants Returning to their Home Countries, but Effectiveness of Reintegration Efforts Remains to Be Determined*. [9]

www.ingramcontent.com/pod-product-compliance
Lightning Source LLC
Chambersburg PA
CBHW080619270326
41928CB00016B/3123